MEMORIE

Warwickshire Coalfields

David Bell

COUNTRYSIDE BOOKS
NEWBURY BERKSHIRE

First published 2011
© David Bell 2011

COUNTRYSIDE BOOKS
3 Catherine Road
Newbury, Berkshire

To view our complete range of books,
please visit us at
www.countrysidebooks.co.uk

ISBN 978 1 84674 262 0

Designed by Peter Davies, Nautilus Design

Produced through MRM Associates Ltd., Reading
Typeset by CJWT Solutions, St Helens
Printed by Cambridge University Press

Contents

Acknowledgements

I **wish to express my thanks** to the people at the Coal Authority archives at Berry Hill for all their help. I would also like to thank Bill Joyce, Howard Baker, Ken Lewis, John Moffat, Peter Goodridge, Malcolm Beck, Everard Emery, Nick Roe, Goff Lewis, Russ Guy, Chris Jones, Roy and Rosemary Jones, Elaine Clayton and Dr David Clarke MBE.

4

MAP SHOWING THE WARWICKSHIRE COALFIELDS IN 1957

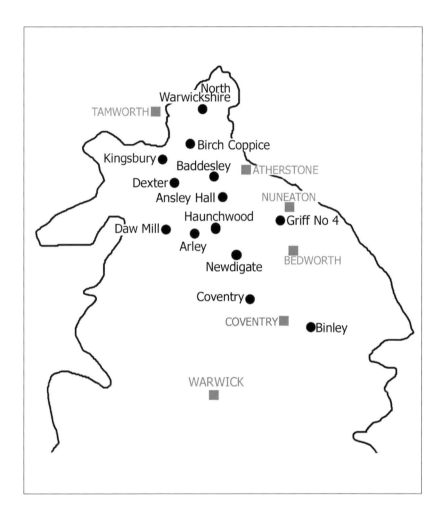

Introduction

The **Warwickshire coalfield covers** some 385 square kilometres and stretches from Tamworth in the north to Warwick in the south. The towns of Tamworth, Atherstone, Nuneaton and Bedworth, as well as the city of Coventry, all lie within the coalfield area. Although Tamworth is now entirely in Staffordshire, the Warwickshire-Staffordshire border once ran through the middle of the town, putting half of Tamworth in Warwickshire. In 1888, it was decided that the town should be entirely within one county, and in a close-run headcount – 2,589 to 2,032 – it went into Staffs. Many Tamworth townspeople, however, still feel great affinity with their Warwickshire neighbours.

The Warwickshire coalfield has been worked since the 13th century, particularly in the northern end of the coalfield, where the coal lies close to the surface. Because it was so easy to reach, it was the earliest part of Warwickshire to be mined, in shallow bell pits at first, then by horse gins. The bell pits were vertical shafts that widened into a bell shape at the bottom. These were worked by a two-man team, one man descending a ladder to reach the coal, and sending it to the surface in a bucket winched up by his comrade, in the same way as water from a well. Each bell pit was soon worked out and a new one had to be dug. When slightly deeper coal was to be mined, the only way to winch it to the surface was by means of a horse walking in a circle, with a rope over a drum into the shaft below. The shallow coal could also be reached by an adit – a drift running horizontally or at a slope into a hillside.

Many of the early miners were monks, in fact, and there are several stories connected with the old mining monks. Bill

Joyce, who was a miner at Coventry pit in Keresley, told me, 'There's dozens and dozens of old pits round here, old monks' workings.'

Bill went on to tell me about a colleague who accidentally discovered some old workings from the days of the monk-miners. 'This chap had worked at a pit over in Arley. He was cutting one morning, and the ground collapsed underneath him. He fell down about ten foot, cutter and all. No one was hurt, just cuts and bruises, but when they looked round where they had landed, it was a proper tunnel, bricked all the way round. It was an old monks' coalmine. They'd been working over the top of it, and the weight of the cutter had gone through. He said that there was a long groove in the side, a channel running all the way along the wall, about two inches in diameter. It was covered over with clay. The monks could only go so far in, you see, and that groove in the wall was their air supply. That's how they used to get the air through to them.'

In the early days coal was transported from the pits by horse and cart, but in the late 18th and early 19th century, canals were built, and these proved ideal for moving coal. They could take heavy loads with ease and, because coal was not a cargo that would deteriorate, speed of travel was not a problem. My nephew, Chris Jones, has traced his maternal roots back to the Barlow family, who were Warwickshire canal boat people. The Samuel Barlow Coal Company Ltd moved coal by canal in the area for many generations, with branches in Birmingham, Coventry and Tamworth. Even when the railways came along, the canal transporters could undercut their new competitors, where speed of delivery was not a factor. In fact, many Warwickshire collieries would take the coal to the canal wharf by train, then load it onto the Barlow barges. In the 20th century, the Samuel Barlow Coal Company Ltd merged with another local coal delivery firm to become Barlow and Willday, and used lorries to take the coal to its customers.

When the country's coalmines were nationalised in 1947, there were nineteen collieries in the Warwickshire coalfield. This

The Samuel Barlow Coal Company delivered coal from Warwickshire pits by canal.

A pair of Barlow boats about to be loaded at Baddesley Wharf.

The Samuel Barlow Coal Company later turned to road deliveries.

number diminished, Hawkesbury closing in 1948 and Griff Clara in 1955. Three pits – Pooley Hall, Alvecote and Amington – merged to form a single pit called North Warwickshire colliery in 1951, so by 1957, ten years after nationalisation, there were just twelve. The total number of miners employed at these twelve collieries was 16,754. The largest was Coventry – often called Keresley pit, because it was actually situated at Keresley – with 2,407 men. The smallest two were Ansley Hall and Haunchwood, and these merged into one pit – Haunchwood – in 1959.

However, at the same time as these pits were closing, a new one was being started. Its first shaft was actually a ventilation shaft at Dexter colliery, and it was sunk in 1957–59, and a second shaft was added in 1969–71. This new pit, Daw Mill, quickly overtook its neighbour in terms of importance, mining a five-metre high section of the Warwickshire Thick seam some 750 metres below the ground. In 1982, a drift entrance was completed so that coal could be brought to the surface via an inclined tunnel. This

9

Ansley Hall colliery. (National Archives)

enabled Daw Mill to increase production capacity by removing the bottleneck of winding coal up the shafts.

Daw Mill is now owned by a company called UK Coal. When the country's few remaining pits were privatised in 1994, they were bought by RJB Mining – sometimes informally called Budge, after its owner Richard J. Budge. On the retirement of Richard Budge in 2001, the company became known by its present name. Remarkably, Daw Mill is one of only three deep mines that are still producing coal today. It is Britain's most productive pit, fully mechanised and computerised, and it employs over 600 men. These come from a very wide area, travelling to work from distant parts. Ev Emery told me, 'It's all changed now. At one time, it was the village and the pit. If you didn't walk to work, you could bike it. But now it's come to a point where down Daw Mill you see people you don't even know. That never happened before.' His friend Malc Beck added, 'Some of these people are

Haunchwood colliery: the headgear, October 1965.
(National Archives)

Daw Mill. The two men are 'thurling' – making an entrance to another roadway, June 1982. (National Archives)

Daw Mill: four-ton mine cars in the main roadway in pit bottom circuit. (National Archives)

Daw Mill: monorail transport system. (National Archives)

A commemorative plate showing the Warwickshire pits.

travelling sixty or seventy miles from the top end of Nottinghamshire.'

As pits closed in both Warwickshire and other mining areas, many miners came to work at Daw Mill, but there was one exception. When Coventry pit at Keresley closed in 1991, the owners of Daw Mill would not take any of the men. The reason? Coventry miners had supported the Great Strike of 1984–5, and Daw Mill had not. Coventry men had remained in the National Union of Miners, and Daw Mill wanted only men who were in the newly-formed Union of Democratic Mineworkers (UDM). However, this may have been relaxed slightly; I do know of at least one NUM member working at Daw Mill.

Chapter 1

Starting Work

One of the most important moments in life is the transition from school to work. One day, you are an important person at school – one of the older pupils – but the next you are the 'new boy' at work, a youngster surrounded by adults. And for the miner, this transition has an extra element. You go from the surface to the underground, from the sunlight to the dark. The first trip down in the cage is a life-changing journey. And even if you coped with the descent, you then had to proceed further into the mine.

Coventry miner Bill Joyce told me, 'The first time down the shaft didn't bother me, but it did some people. Out of every twelve people that came to Coventry colliery for prospective jobs, ten or eleven of them would pack up in the first day or the first week. It was not so much the going down, but when they start to get further under they feel that it closes in on them, that's what did it.'

Perhaps one of the reasons Bill coped with his first journey in the cage might be the fact that he was 21 years old, and had been in

*Going down in the cage
at Haunchwood.*

the army. He explained, 'I went down the pit in 1948, when I came out the army – demobbed. I lived with my grandmother and grandfather. My grandfather worked at Dunlop, and coming home one night at seven o'clock, something hit him, a lorry or something. The poor old bugger got knocked out, and he was out there all night.' With his grandfather out of action, this left Bill as the sole breadwinner, and he got demobbed on those grounds. He told me, 'I was the house supporter, so I come out of the army on a class B, which meant I had to go down the pit or work on a farm for eighteen months. I didn't fancy the farm, so I thought I'd do eighteen months down the pit. But I stayed at Coventry pit nearly forty years.'

John Moffat was much younger when he went down the pit. 'I went down the pit in 1970 at Baddesley – the mother pit. That's where my heart is and always will be. I was fifteen. Everybody

Coventry colliery: men on the underground transport.
(National Archives)

started at Birch Coppice training centre. There's thousands gone through Birch Coppice. They had everything there – it was a proper training set-up. There was a gym, football in the afternoon. It was like a school, really, a proper school.

'I was probably about sixteen, my first trip down in the cage. What you'd got at Baddesley was an eight-man cage, and there was two shafts, and they were only about ten foot apart. Eight men on wooden cages. At the time I started, they had the old keps underneath. It would come up to the landing, and they'd pull the keps up, and lock them. The cage sat on that. But they had to take them away because sometimes people forgot to take them out, and the rope would start to come down, and then it was struggling to pull it out and people was shouting. That was no 1 and no 2 shafts, and then the main shaft was the winding shaft for the coal.'

John had four years at Baddesley pit and then he decided he

Baddesley colliery coalface. (National Archives)

wanted to see a bit of the world. 'I started as a mining craft apprentice and went through the system. I was at Baddesley from 1970 to 1974, and then I left. I went into the Merchant Navy for two years, but then I met Linda when I was on leave, and I didn't go back. The Merchant Navy was sort of winding down at that time, going under flags of convenience to make it cheaper. It had become harder to find ships and work, so I went back to Baddesley colliery. I seen the training officer, Eddie Baxter, and he set me straight back on.'

When I asked John about his first time down, he denied that he had any qualms. 'No I wasn't nervous. To be honest, you've got no fear when you're that age. No fear of nothing. You can do anything.' However, John added that, today, he has fewer feelings of immortality. 'I'm probably a bit more cautious now, especially when I go down on my own at Daw Mill. There's guides on there, and there's bends in the shaft. Sometimes it feels like it's faster than it should be, especially when you're on your own, and you think, "This is going a bit quick." But no, it's never really bothered me. I suppose it would if I'd ever had an incident on it.'

Howard Baker went into the mining industry in 1950 when he was sixteen, but he went in by accident. He told me, 'I was in the Sixth Form at Atherstone Grammar School and, of course, in those days, you never had anybody come and talk to you about any careers whatsoever. And the staff didn't talk to you about careers neither. They might have done if you were the son or daughter of a solicitor or a doctor, but I never got any.

'I'd developed an interest in ordnance surveying, so I wrote off to the Ordnance Survey, and they said that they wanted some qualifications. I also wrote to the Admiralty, the hydrography department, and they said I was too young at 16 but to contact them again in a year's time.

'My father, who was a pitman at Kingsbury and Dexter, said, 'Why don't you go to the pit and get a job on the survey staff for a year. Don't tell them, just go and get a job. So off I went, this Saturday morning, on my bike up to Kingsbury colliery. I saw the office manager and said I'd come for a job. He said, "The only jobs we've got are on the screens." Well, I didn't know what screens were, but I didn't like the sound of it. So I stood on the doorstep, a bit nonplussed, and then he said, "What school did you go to?" I said, "Atherstone Grammar School." "Have you got a school certificate?" "Yes I have." I'm on the doorstep, talking to him. Then he said, "What did you say your surname was?" "Baker." "Does your dad work here? Is he a ginger-haired chap, Stan Baker?" "Yes." "Ah, I'll tell you what, I'll go and have a word with the manager." Off he went, then came back and said, "Mr Mawbey would like you to come in and see him."

'So I went in to see Mr Mawbey, and he was an ex-army officer who'd come back into the industry. He said to me, "Why do you want to go on the survey?" So I thought the last thing I was going to do was tell him. So I made some sort of reply, and he says, "What was your school certificate results?" I told him, and I explained that I was a year early taking my certificate, so I was now in the Sixth Form, but I didn't really want to do French and the other subjects. He said, "Ah, how would you like to be an under-manager?" I didn't know what an under-manager was, but it sounded a bit better than working on the screens. So I said, "I might be interested in that." He says, "I understand your dad works here. Why don't you go home and have a word with him. Tell him I'm suggesting that you train to be an under-manager. Then you can come back and see Mr Bidulph and you can start." So I got on my bike and went off to Wilnecote and sounded my dad out. He said, "Yes, why don't you." So that were it.

'The first time I went down the pit would be at the training centre at Birch Coppice. Warwickshire used to have a training centre at Wood End, but it was all part of Birch Coppice colliery, so that was probably where I went down the first time. That was in the age of the steam winder, and if anybody gave the winder a thumb-up as they were taking us across to the pit top, telling them there were some first-timers with them, it was a fast drop for the first few feet.'

Another Atherstone Grammar School student was Peter Goodridge. Like Howard, Peter came from a mining background.

A shearer at the coalface. (National Archives)

He is very proud of his ancestry and told me, 'I have been connected with the coalmining industry for most of my life, directly or indirectly. I come from a coalmining family. My dad worked down Baddesley pit for most of his life, with a break of four years when he served in the army during the First World War. The first generation was my grandfather, who died before I was born. The second was my dad and his brother, my Uncle Tom, and the third was Tom's son, my cousin Arthur. Tom and his sons also worked at Baddesley pit all their working lives, and my brother and I both worked in the industry for about fifteen years each.'

Peter showed me an extract from Laurence Fretwell's book *The Warwickshire Coalfield*, which refers to Speedwell shaft, about half a mile from Baddesley colliery's main shaft. The extract states: This platform cage was only ever used once a day for man-riding, by a man whose job it was to inspect the water level and shaft installations. This job was traditionally done by a member of the Gutteridge family who for three generations fulfilled this task.'

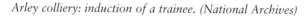

Arley colliery: induction of a trainee. (National Archives)

Baddesley colliery. (National Archives)

Peter explained that the Gutteridge family is actually his own Goodridge family. He said, 'The mis-spelling of our name makes me think that Laurence Fretwell actually obtained this information verbally, as Goodridge is often mispronounced in this way. The part of the mine where they worked was called the Water Level, and they were known as the Water Rats, or in the Baddesley dialect the "Wayter Rots". They performed an essential task in keeping the roadway clear and the water pumped out, which if neglected would have led to flooding problems in other parts of the pit.'

Peter continued: 'I first went down the pit in 1951, on my eighteenth birthday. I was at Atherstone Grammar School, and I went into the Sixth Form, doing 'A' levels, but I was interested in poultry even then. I'd got a Saturday job on a poultry farm, and there was a lad there named Bill Bostock who was a couple of years older than me. He had to leave to go and do his National Service, and I was offered his job. So, very unwisely, I left school at Easter 1950 and gave up the possibility of going to university to work full-time on the poultry farm.

'I was coming up to my eighteenth birthday, and there were two alternatives: either go and do my National Service – which I didn't want to do because I'd got quite a big poultry holding going at home – or go down the pit. I decided to go down the pit.

'I'd been working for probably two months on the surface at Baddesley colliery, because the system then was that the youngsters, the school leavers, went to college for one or two days a week, and they worked on the surface until they finished their training and then they went underground. But the other system was – for eighteen plus – you did three weeks' training at Wood End training pit, which was an upcast shaft for Birch Coppice. So Harold Thorpe, the training officer, said that as I was only a few weeks away from my eighteenth birthday, I could work on the surface until then, and then do the three weeks' training course. So my first journey down the pit was at Wood End. I did the three weeks' training course there, then I went down Baddesley.

Malcolm Beck said, 'I started on 10th August 1970, at Newdigate colliery as an apprentice electrician. But the first time down the shaft was obviously at Birch Coppice, the training pit. You go on the cage and you think, "Oh, I don't know whether I'm going to like this!" You don't know whether you're going to suffer from claustrophobia. When he drops that gate and then he shuts the other gate, then he rings three off with the bells, and you think, "Oh my god. Well, that's it now. Too late now."

'You start descending slowly down into the abyss, and it gets darker. You can feel the warm air rushing up. Then it starts getting quicker and quicker. You think, "How far is this going to go?" All of a sudden it slows right down. But you're only down at the Seven-Foot level, which is probably only a hundred metres down, not that deep at all. The cage stops, and it springs a bit in the shaft. You think, "Is this it, then? That's not very far." But you don't realise that's only the training area. You get off there, and then the cage disappears without you and goes further down. You think, "Oh no, it does carry on then. What's it like right down there?"

'You walk into this training area and it's all whitewashed,

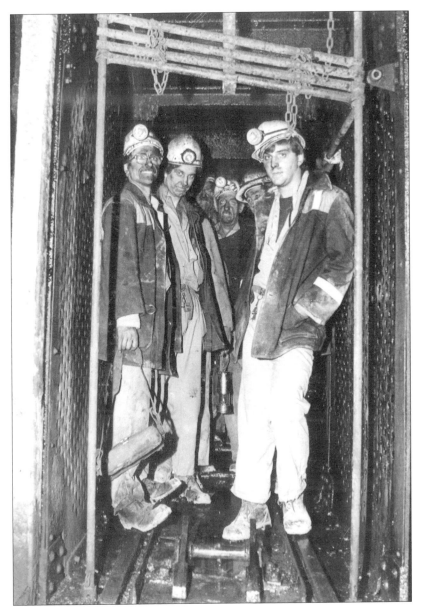

Newdigate colliery: miners about to descend in the cage. (National Archives)

Arley colliery: Training Officer Bobby Grant provides induction training. (National Archives)

Ansley Hall colliery: apprentices in the training centre. (National Archives)

everything looks pristine and smart. Then you go and sit down on this bench and the instructor says, "Right, this is what we're going to do today, and this is the training area." Obviously you'd gone through all the self-rescue and everything. And then you start walking down this hill. It was a good way down the South Bench hill at Birch Coppice. You come to this low bit, and the instructor says, "Right, we're going to build this wooden pillar to hold the roof up. This is how you do it." He starts getting these wooden chocks, and he lays them in fours and then twos. He says, "You do the same then." Of course you're all building one – there's four of you on each pillar. You're all trying to beat each other. When you get to the top, he says, "Right, now then, you've got to make sure this is tight to the roof for obvious reasons." He starts getting timps – wedges – and you start knocking them in with a hammer so it's really tight to the roof. He looks at the other ones, and they've not quite built it as neat, because they were trying to do it too quick, and he says, "That's no good. If the weight come on there, them blocks going to fly out of there. You've got to make sure it's in tight, and square." He's putting you right all the time. 'You think, "Oh my god, I don't know if I'm going to take to this. I thought I was an electrician and now I'm building bloody wooden blocks." But obviously you have to learn to do it.'

Malcolm's colleague Everard Emery chipped in, 'I remember when I first went down Haunchwood pit. It was at Easter 1955. Haunchwood was an old pit, years old. They'd worked out what they called the Nine Foot seam, and they'd gone down into the Bench. The first time I went down the pit, we went down in the cage and we went down past the old pit bottom! The old area was all lit up, and we saw it as we went by it. The shaft went down another fifty yards to the very bottom, but we didn't know about that, did we. We went down to the very bottom. And of course, when I was starting, it was all steam winding. They used to go a bit faster than the later electric winding.'

Ev's story is a remarkable one. He went down the pit at the age of fifteen, and now in his seventies he is still working in a colliery. Not many miners can claim a working career of over fifty-five

Haunchwood miners climbing the steps to the cage.

Going down in the cage at Haunchwood.

The underground loco roadway at Haunchwood colliery.
(National Archives)

years! He explained, 'I had twelve years at Haunchwood colliery, then came the 1960s when the cheap oil came in and the pits started to close. So we went to Arley colliery, which was going to be the be-all and end-all. But I was there for only twelve months and that one closed. So I went from twelve years at Haunchwood to twelve months at Arley. I then went to Newdigate in 1968 until that pit closed in 1982, and I then moved to Daw Mill. And I'm still there. I've worked at four pits. I'm 71 now, so I don't think I'll do another one!'

Chapter 2

Nicknames and Banter

One aspect of pit humour was the banter that went on between the miners. Everyone wanted to have the last word, to come back with a witty put-down. And it was even better if you were dealing with an official: a deputy or an overman.

Malcolm Beck gave me an example of an exchange between a miner nicknamed Creamy and Ernie Day, the overman. 'Ernie Day used to walk up and say, "What y'doing?" That's how he used to talk to us. He ruled Newdigate pit but he were a great bloke. He hadn't got any friends in the world – he used to talk to everybody the same – but if he gave you a bollocking, that's as far as it went. He'd say to people, "What y'doing? What y'supposed to be doing? Why aren't y'doing it then?" That's how he used to talk to people.

'Now this Creamy was on a belt delivery, and he was always there cleaning up. That was his job. He used to run the switches at the face as well. One time, Ernie Day come along, and there was a pile of coal, and Creamy was sat in this man-hole reading a paper. Of course, Ernie Day walked up to Creamy and he's seen

Daw Mill colliery. (National Archives)

this pile of coal on the plough. He says, "Have y'got a shovel?" And Creamy says, "Yes. Help yourself, but bring it back when you've done." Of course, what Ernie meant was, "Get it bloody cleaned up."

'Creamy was on the face switches once, and of course some places down the pit, it's a bit cold. But the transformer were that big, they're nice and warm. Especially on nights, you could go and have a minute – have a lie down – on the top of them. Of course, Creamy were up there on top of this bloody transformer having a minute – and he was supposed to be running the switches. Ernie Day come through the face, and in them days we always used to have warnings on the tannoys. They used to come out with different codes to let you know the gaffer were coming. Anyway,

Newdigate colliery: at the coalface. (National Archives)

Creamy couldn't hear the warnings, up on this transformer. Then, sure enough, Ernie Day comes through and he couldn't find Creamy. Next thing, he looks up and sees him lying on top of this transformer. Ernie turns round to him and he says, "Are y'comfortable?" And Creamy looked at him and he says, "I could do with a blanket." Which is not what you're supposed to say to the colliery overman. Mind you, they were both on nights regular, so Creamy knew Ernie Day, and Ernie knew Creamy. He'd worked with him all his life, and he let him get away with so much.'

Banter could also come out in song! Peter Goodridge told about a miner who was paying maintenance to a girl in Hartshill whom he had got into trouble a few years earlier. 'When he got behind with his payments, she used to get the police on to him. I think she must have known someone in the Force, because I doubt whether the police would have concerned themselves with such matters, even in those days. He used to come into work with a long face, saying, "The boys in blue have been down again." We used to sing the song *Who's Sorry Now?* to him, and there was a great crescendo when we got to the lines *You had your way, now you must pay*. His wife used to give him hell, and who could blame her if she was short on the housekeeping and he was having to fork out money to pay for his earlier indiscretions.'

The act of coming out with banter was so ingrained that it would come out without any forethought. Bill Joyce recalled two occasions when he did just that. 'We were working on a place about eighteen inches high, and this bloke slipped and fell. Down he went, bang! Bang! Hitting the sides. He was groaning. "You all right?" "Course I'm bloody not," he said. "I fell on my head." I said, "Christ you were lucky. And don't tell the manager or he'll be suing you for damage." It just come out, without thinking, you know.

'I remember another time, there was a big lump of coal – it'd be two tons – and it had fell, rolled, and pinned this bloke. We were working about fifty yards from him, and when I came out there was two of his mates on top, one with a hammer and one with a pick. They were about five foot above him and he was underneath. I said, "Get off! What are you doing?" They said, "Jock's underneath." I said, "Well, get off there, you're only putting extra weight on him." I had a look and of course there was gummins under him – slack and coal dirt. I said, "You go for a stretcher, and you get a tree and get down there with me. We'll get a fulcrum, put the tree on it to rest the weight a little bit. We'll shovel underneath his body and his feet. When we think he's clear, one pull and we'll drag him out." He was trapped up to his chest. Not thinking, I said to Jock, "Stop there while I get this tree." As if he had any choice! He was that mad, he picked a piece of coal and threw it at me. What I meant was "Don't start struggling" but what I said was "Stop there", which he didn't think was funny. Anyway we managed to get him out. A tree, by the way, was a wooden pit prop.'

Bill continued, 'Everyone was a character in his own way. We were talking about one lad. Televisions had just come out – 9 ins or 12 ins screen, I think they were. This lad said, "Oh I've got an 16 inch television." The others said, "Oh, you liar." "I have, I tell you. The wife's got herself a job. We've saved up, and we've paid £5 deposit and £1 a week." One of his mates said, "I wouldn't have one like that." He said, "Why wouldn't you? They look after it all." His mate replied, "I want to pay for it and know it's mine. And then if I want to smash it up, I can smash it up." "Yeah, that's just about what you bleddy would do," he says.'

One aspect of miners' banter and chat was the telling of tall tales. Ev Emery told me, 'Jeff Parsons was a big allotment man. He could tell some stories. One was about when a rabbit was eating all his lettuce. He was fed up with it and he said, "I'm gonna get a gun." He said, "I got the gun and I went up the allotment. I sat there and these two ears appeared over the lettuce. I shot it, but it turned out to be the farmer's donkey." He was bragging how big his lettuces were. He used to get everybody listening to his tales.'

The allotment stories must have been a regular source of tall tales because Bill Joyce said, 'There were some characters at Coventry pit, and we used to have a laugh about allotments and gardening. A chap called Dick Barton said to us, "I'll tell you what. We've got some old manure, really old. It's been there two year. The farmer gave me half a load, and I've put it up there at the bottom end of the garden. I'd got my potatoes in, and they looked good. I got my fork under them and it creaked. There was twenty-eight pound of potatoes on it. It nearly broke the fork."

'And there was Swimmer, he was the best. He could tell 'em all day. He was sitting down having his snap, and there were about eight or nine people there. They was all having their bread. Swimmer says, "I went to London to see the match Saturday. It was a good match, but I didn't see it all. I had to come out just after half-time. I had to come home." I said, "Why? What was the matter?" "Well," he says, "you know the wife was expecting?" "Yes," I said, "I didn't think you'd go to the match." "Well," he says, "we'd got the tickets booked. It was all paid for and she said, 'Go on. I'll be all right.' So we went. Well, you know that blue chequered pigeon I've got? My best one. Well, I looked up and there it was circling above me. There were 80,000 people there, but it spotted me and dropped on me shoulder. There was a little note on the leg, and it said, 'Come home. Water's broke!'"

'Swimmer always knew more facts than anyone else,' Bill went on. 'Swimmer was talking to a man, and he said, "Can a lion swim?" "Yeah, lions can swim." "Well they can't cos their manes get too heavy." Well, can a pig swim? "No cos their feet come up and cuts their throat." He says, "That's where you get that black pudding from."' Bill explained how Swimmer got his nickname, 'He reckoned he dived in the canal at Nuneaton, and he come out at Atherstone, about four mile away. He said there was a tunnel underneath and he swam underwater all the way.'

Nicknames were a regular feature of life in the pits. They were especially useful when there were several members of the same family working together, brothers or fathers and sons. You might not know Joe Smith from Jack Smith or Bill Smith, but you *would* know Tubby from Titch or Smiler. John Moffat recalled, 'Oh yes, there were thousands of nicknames. At Baddesley, there was Ferret. And at Daw Mill, there was Bin Dog and Mosher. There were some good old lads.'

Peter Goodridge remembered, 'There was Brian Barsby, known as Mush, and Howard Dennis whose nickname was Custard. Dennis Bartlam was known as Cherry and Stan Temple was nicknamed Cluey. Another member of the gang was Mick Morris, whose dad was known for making a hole in each end of

Coventry colliery: setting rings in a gate. (National Archives)

a hen's egg and sucking out and swallowing the contents. Predictably, his nickname was Suckegg, often shortened to Suckie. Mick had inherited his dad's nickname and was also known as Suckie.'

Bill Joyce commented, 'There's no sympathy down the pit, you know. There was one we called Bulldog, there was Groupy-face and Hangdog, another was Squinty. Then there was Brutex – he had a flat nose.' Bill laughed when he recalled how he'd given one man a new nickname. 'We used to put these sixteen foot rings in, and this chap was short of bolts to fasten the plates to the rings. He'd come from the tail gate end, about a hundred yards away, and he came to us for some bolts. We'd given him what we'd got spare. But while we was having our snap, he come back and pinched some more. So I called him Boltneck. And it stuck. We were at the club one night, and he was there with his wife, and somebody shouted across to him, "Hey Boltneck!" He turns to me and he says, "That's your fault, that is, you bastard. Everybody's calling me Boltneck now."'

Ken Lewis came to Coventry pit from his native South Wales in 1966, when he was in his mid-thirties, and worked there until he retired in 1985. Ken put his reminiscences into verse. As you will see, the tall tales of the allotment crop up again.

> *When you first started work your training began*
> *How to use a big shovel and pick*
> *The old ones would ask you 'What is your name?'*
> *To find a nickname that would stick.*
>
> *A nickname would stick for the rest of your days*
> *Clive Rose, they nicknamed him Petal.*
> *My grandfather played a side drum in a band*
> *So they gave him the name of Kettle.*

Ron Rat caught rats as a hobby
His nickname was not very nice.
They thought up a name for Tom Thomas
And decided to call him Tom Twice.

Dai Cabbage got his for tales that he told
He was a gardener devout
He went down his plot to cut cabbage one day
He shook one and two sheep fell out!

I remember our overman, Jack Eighteen-months
How he got his name still makes me laugh
A stone fell and cut his ear off, they say
So it left him an 'ear and a half'.

The nicknames were so prevalent that often people wouldn't even know the real names. Ev Emery commented, 'On nights, I used to be in charge because there was no chargehand so the fitter would take charge. Ernie Day, the overman, got me on the phone. He says, "There's a woman on the phone wants to know if Gordon Reveley's there. I've told her there's no such person works here." I said, "Yes, there is. That's Creamy." He says, "Oh, is it?" This overman, Ernie Day, was the man who was booking the men in, and even he didn't know Creamy's real name. Everybody just knew him as Creamy. Hardly anybody knew Creamy was Gordon Reveley.'

It was just the same at Keresley, as Coventry pit was often called. Bill Joyce recalled, 'One particular incident, the gaffer came and said to me, "Bill, I want you to split your team." At that particular time we were tunnelling, road making, sixteen foot high by eighteen foot wide. He wanted me to split the team up and go to another place because there was a fall. He said, "We'll put some extra men in, but you'll have two each of your team with two others to do a four shift." He said, "You select the men, and tell 'em which you're putting on which shift." Well, in the lamp cabin, they had a system there. You'd got a little note on the lamp number. So I put these numbers out. I'm looking at them, thinking, "I don't know him, I don't know him, he's a stranger. He'll go afternoons, he'll go nights." The next morning, one of me old pals come up and said, "Hey, I've gotta go nights." I said, "You haven't got to go nights. I put the notes out." I hadn't recognised the name Gallagher. We always called him Bliss, but I didn't know his name was Gallagher. No one knew his real name. He was just called Bliss.'

Chapter 3

'I Worked With This Character ...'

Many of the miners' reminiscences I listened to began 'I worked with this character ...'. They went on to tell me about men who were eccentric, others who were rough, some who liked a drink, but all were described as being great characters.

Malc Beck and Ev Emery told me more about Creamy, who worked with them at Newdigate colliery. Malc said, 'I never knew Creamy's proper name, but every Friday morning, we used to get us wages. Creamy would go and get his wage packet. It used to have a staple through it, with your money in notes. Straightaway he'd get the staple out and it'd be a fiver under his hat, a fiver up that sleeve, a fiver down that sock. He used to have to riddle his money, then he'd give the wage packet to his wife with less than half of what should have been in there. Even on the bus, he used

Miners collecting their pay.

to sit at the back, putting another fiver down his sock. Harry used to say, "Are you riddling, Creamy?" He say, "Shut up," and he'd carry on. It was so funny. Every Friday morning without fail, he'd put half his money down his sock and up his jumper and under his cap. He was a lovely chap though.'

Ev added, 'The last time I seen Creamy, I went in the town and there he is in a wheelchair. He sat there talking to Jeff Parsons, and this is in the middle of town on a Saturday, and he shouts, "Ev, we want a fitter over here. We've got a cobble in the tension end." Unbelievable.'

Jeff Parsons was another character in his own right. Ev explained, 'Jeff was a prize fighter in the bare-knuckle boxing booths. His dad used to take him all round – and take all the bloody prizes off him. Jeff always used to get an audience when he was telling us about when he fought the championship for the Coal Board – and he used to do all the actions as well. He says, "I fought a chap who was a hard hitter. I only hit him once. He was a nice chap though, because he come to see me in hospital!" He had two allotments, and he used to sell half the stuff for the Heart Foundation.'

Malc told me, 'He could use his fists but I've never known him to get angry. But there were one day down the pit, he were on the tag, on the haulage. He'd got a couple of blokes with him, and one was this young lad named Tommy – he come from Bedworth. He'd be about eighteen. Well the tubs used to come off regular, and they'd have to stop the haulage and lift the tubs back on. It were regular that Jeff used to be the one doing the lifting back on. This Tommy, while Jeff were bending down, he used to give him a sly punch. Jeff said, "Ey, pack it in." Well this went on time and time again, this young lad jabbing Jeff at the wrong time – when he were doing something. This particular day, Jeff was just lifting a tub back on and Tommy does no more, he just punches Jeff straight in the ribs. Jeff stood up and hit him once. He only hit him once with a short jab to the chin, but he knew where to hit him. This Tommy went spark out. Jeff went, "Oh my god." He was trying to bring him round with water and everything. The

'Pikrose' haulage at Birch Coppice colliery. (National Archives)

youth was spark out on the floor. It frit Jeff a bit, and he thought, "What have I done?" But I'll tell you what: this youth never ever hit Jeff again. It was a warning shot across his bows.'

Quite a few of the miners could box. Howard Baker told me, 'There was a pub in Bedworth called Alty's because of the guy who owned it – and they had a boxing club upstairs. In the 1950s they had some very good useful lads on the boxing scene. They used to turn out, from the Bedworth area, one or two useful guys who fought in the Midland ABA championships and they even fought for English titles. Quite a few of the guys from Newdigate colliery used to go up there as sparring partners They earned a pound, or a pint or two. I always remember the story I was told, where they'd been up there one day. They comes outside and started to walk home – they'd had a few pints, as well – and there's a Co-op horse pulling the milk float. And one of them says to the other, "I bet you couldn't shlock him." And he did! The horse was eating his oats, and he just whacked him straight in the stomach and run off.' I'm sorry Howard, but I'm on the horse's side in this one!

It wasn't just the men who were keen on a scrap. Howard had a manager who would have liked to have been in a mêlée. 'We went to a St John's Ambulance presentation at the Working Men's Club at Binley – the Miners Welfare. The manager was there, the group manager, some of the engineers, and the union people. All of a sudden, on the dance floor, there is such a shout. Probably somebody had eyed somebody else's bird, that sort of thing, or eyed somebody's dancing partner. All of a sudden, there was a most wonderful fight. I've never seen one like it. It happened in an instant. There was blokes piling into each other all over the floor. There was guys scuffling all over this floor, and I'll never forget, there was women walking round, they took their high heels off and they was thrashing these blokes. "Hey you, leave my man alone." Hitting each other and going like mad. What a fight that was. They were being knocked all over the shop. We kept edging up to the side of the room. Oh dear. I'd never seen a fight like that ever before in my life. There must have been thirty or forty, all having a go at each other in the end. My manager, Mr Elter, said, "I wish I could go and get into that lot." He loved it! Sadly, he died some time later in a mining accident.' (See Chapter 4.)

Malcolm Beck told me about another hard case, a man named Hughie Barras. 'He was a Scotch fellow, real broad Scotch. We were on nights this particular night. If you smoked, before you went into the airlock you'd stand outside and have a last fag. The spotlights off the headgear would be lighting all the yard up, and you'd be standing there in the cold for ten minutes having a last fag before you went down the pit. There was a bunch of blokes all stood outside having a fag, and this Hughie Barras turned to the bloke next to him and he says, "I could crack your ribs, you know, if I put my arms round you and squeezed." This bloke said, "No you couldn't." At which point, Hughie locked his arms round him, and squeezed. This bloke yelled, "Ahhhh," and dropped to the floor. He was going, "Oh me chest, me chest! He's broke me ribs." Somebody runs up the ambulance room and the medical bloke came running across the yard with the trolley. Ernie Day, the colliery overman, comes out the office and down to all these blokes who were lifting this chap onto the trolley. Ernie says, "What's up? What y'done then?" He says, "I told Hughie he wouldn't be able to crack me ribs. But he did." Ernie Day just looked at this Hughie Barras as if to say, "I can't believe what I'm hearing." But he had, he'd bust his ribs.

'This same Hughie Barras, I grew up with his sons. He were on day shift this particular day and his wife had gone to bed a bit early and she was reading a book in bed. Hughie Barras went to the toilet and then went and got in bed. At which point he said, "Turn that light off." And his missus said, "You've just walked past the light switch. You turn it off." He says, "You were reading the book. You turn the light off." She said, "I am not getting out this bed to turn the light off. You can do it." At which point Hughie leaned across, grabbed her book and threw it at the light bulb. It smashed, glass all over the bed. He said, "Well that's the light out now," and turned over – with the bed covered in bits of glass bulb. That was Hughie Barras. What a character.'

John Moffat told me about a man he worked with at Baddesley pit named Vic. 'There was one character called Vic de Silver but we called him Vic de Moulder. When he come out the pit he looked like a panda. I used to work at the stable with him, and I could see him chewing. I thought, "He's got sweets and he ain't saying anything." I said, "Come on Vic. Get the sweets out." He said, "I ain't got no sweets." So I said, "What are you chewing then?" He'd got a face full of it – and he was chewing coal. And he also used to take the red plastic caps out the hoses and he chewed on them, an' all. He was a scratter for snap. He'd pick anybody's snap up. They used to stop for snap, and chuck the crusts on the face chain. And when he got to the stable he used to pick the crusts up and eat them!'

One or two of the characters were known to have too much to drink. Ev told me about two men he worked with at Haunchwood

---

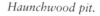

Haunchwood pit.

pit. 'One was Horace Russell. He lived with his mother. He was a man in his forties but lived with his mother all his life. He used to like a drink. He used to catch the bus by the Malt Shovel at Hartshill. He come out the pub this night, he'd had a skin-full, and he was trying to find his way home. He's standing by the bus stop when the pit bus comes by. They see him, stops, puts him on the bus and takes him to the pit. When he gets out and looks round, he says, "Why am I at the pit. I ain't on nights!"

'Then there was little Greenie. He was a rough lad and he liked a drink as well. His wife says, "You ain't going out for a drink tonight, are you? It's chucking it down with rain." He says, "Well, I went to work in it so I'm going to go out for a drink in it." She said, "If you go out tonight, I'll lock you out." He says, "Please yourself what you do." He goes for a drink and when he comes back, she's locked him out. He said, "I put her right. I went to the garage, got the big hammer and smashed the door down." His wife says, "What about the door?" He says, "I'm not bothered. I'm going to bed." Characters, aren't they?'

Peter Goodridge told me about a Scotsman who'd arrived in Warwickshire, who didn't understand the local miners' dialect. 'This Scotsman came down to Baddesley, and his first day down, the deputy sent him down one of the gates, one of the belt roads, and said, "You'll find some chaps down there baiting. You can join in with them." Anyway, he came back and he said, "I can't find any chaps baiting. There were only some blokes digging the soil out from underneath the belt." The anomaly was that up in Scotland bait is what we call snap down here. So he went down the road, expecting to see chaps sitting, having their bait, having their snap. Down here, baiting means digging the floor out, increasing the height of the roadway. It's also called dinting. I don't know whether baiting is just a Baddesley term for it.

'Then there was Wag Evans. He was the senior day-shift overman, second only to the under-manager. He wore a leather strap round his neck, which he hung his safety lamp on while going through the coalface on his hands and knees. I once heard a fitter unkindly remark that it was a bit like watching Bertram

Arley colliery: pit bottom junctions showing arches and conveyor.
(National Archives)

Mills' circus going past. Like many other miners he chewed tobacco. If you knew Wag was coming round, it would be wise to hide your water bottle. He would have a drink out of any handy bottle, with tobacco juice running down his chin, then take his false teeth out and swill them. If I thought Wag had drunk out of my bottle, I would have died of thirst rather than drink out of it myself. But there was no better pitman anywhere. What Wag didn't know about mining coal wasn't worth knowing.

'I think Johnny Curtis had a screw loose, if not two or three. I remember once needing the hydraulic prop spanner. We used to call it the cockerel's head, because it bore a vague resemblance to one. I shouted to Johnny who was about fifteen yards away to pass it to me. He didn't pass it, he threw it. It bounced once and then hit me on the thigh. I had a bruise the size of a saucer for a week!

'Johnny had a couple of favourite tricks when we were on the way out at the end of a shift. No. 21's main belt was on an uphill incline about three or four hundred yards long. We used to ride the belt, which you could be fined for if an official caught you. I'm sure they rode it themselves if there was no one about. I know I did when I was shot firing. There were such things as man-riding belts with proper boarding and alighting platforms, but there were none of those at Baddesley during my time.

'Halfway up the incline there was a lodgement – a small reservoir into which water was pumped from the bottom of the incline. It is only possible to pump water up to a certain maximum height, hence the need for a lodgement halfway up, where another pump took over to pump the water the rest of the way. Johnny used to run like mad up the belt to the lodgement, where there was an old bucket which he used to ladle as much water as he could onto the belt so the rest of us riding up were met by cascades of water flooding down the belt.

'In the meantime, Johnny had run the rest of the way up to the loader where there was a hose connected to a tap, used to lay the dust. He turned this on full blast to greet us as we got off the belt. We used to hang back until he'd had his bit of fun. One afternoon,

Double-deck man-riding conveyor at Daw Mill. (National Archives)

we were a man short and my brother came with us in his place. At the end of the shift, my brother went on ahead. "You'll get wet," I warned him. He replied, "He wouldn't dare," but Johnny did dare. My brother got wet and he wasn't very pleased, but he couldn't say that we hadn't warned him.'

Malcolm Beck recalled another workmate from Newdigate. 'Our old shift chargehand was a chap named Horace Pitchford, and he'd got the oldest helmet. It was made of compressed cardboard. He'd had it all his life, and he weren't gonna change it. Time and time again, the safety blokes would say, "You've got to get a new helmet. That's not enough." But he still went down the pit with this old helmet on.

'He used to works days and nights, as we used to work then. We used to work Friday nights, but Sunday nights were overtime. Of course, being a young lad and only just married, I used to work Sunday nights for the extra money. I used to pick Horace up and take him to work, bring him back, and drop him off. But he would not come in on Monday morning, when we were back on days. He'd always have Monday mornings off. Without fail. Every Monday morning. But he'd worked the Sunday night, and that's how he looked at it. He'd do the full night shifts, but he'd only do four on days. The gaffer says to him, "Look, Horace we've got to do something about this. You've got to start coming in on Mondays. We can't afford for you to have every Monday off." Horace says, "Well, I work the Sunday nights." The gaffer says, "I know you do and we appreciate that. But you've got to start coming Mondays. I'm really looking to you working Monday next week." Horace turned up on Monday, and when he walked in, everybody clapped. Sure enough, he worked the Monday, but then he didn't in come on the Tuesday. That was Horace.'

Chapter 4

Accidents Did Happen

Every miner I spoke to told me of accidents that he'd witnessed. Most said that they themselves had had no bad injuries, though even then one or two went on to describe what sounded nasty to me. Many pitmen have 'miners' tattoos', blue marks on the arms or bodies caused when coal dust had got into a wound and, despite washing it out in the baths, the wound had healed over the coal dust, leaving a blue mark.

Bill Joyce, telling me about his years as a Coventry miner, remembered, 'Never a week went by without an accident.' He described how one man had undergone great pain without shouting or groaning while Bill got him free. 'One chap had a scraper chain, a belt goes round and loads onto the chain. He was working away to get a prop out, and the prop had fallen onto the chain, and it had stood almost upright, and pinned his hand to the roof. It had acted as a bull stump and stopped the chain. So they sent for me. I said, "What's up?" Blood was dripping down, and we thought, "How are we going to get him out?" Somebody said, "Well, we could reverse the chain." But when you reverse the

A 'casualty' is transported as part of a training exercise at Griff Clara colliery. (National Archives)

chain, before it reverses, it tightens. I said, "That'll take his hand right off." We hadn't got a saw, but I'd got a tadge, an axe. I said, "I've got this, it's pretty sharp." He said, "Get it off, get it done." And he stood there while I chopped through that tree, that prop. It was a 6-inch tree. I chopped through it, to break it, to get his hand out. He never made a sound. He passed out after, but he never made a sound. Marvellous.'

Some miners could stand the pain as long as they thought the injury was minor. Bill continued, 'One lad named Jakey, he had a piece of coal come up and ripped all his shin, peeled it right back to the bone. The deputy came up and got his bandages out, first aid, and cleaned it and wrapped round. He said, "Oh, you've had worse than this, Jake. You'll be all right. Yeah, it's a good job you can stand pain." Jakey says, "Aye, it is, yeah." But then one of Jakey's mates come up and said, "Oh, hell's bells! That looks bad. You'll be off six months." Well, when he heard that, Jakey started groaning something terrible. He'd been okay till then.'

Peter Goodridge recalled an accident that happened to him. 'I was shot firing at Baddesley, and it was the start of the shift. I'd hidden my shot firing gear – my ramming stick, cable, battery – behind the switches. I went to get them, and I must have swung on the switches. These switches weigh several tons, and they must have been on a tilt because they tipped over and pinned me up against one of the arches. My chest was flat! I couldn't shout and I couldn't breathe. Luckily – else I wouldn't be here now – one of the strippers was still in the gate. I just managed to attract his attention and he saw what had happened. He went and got some more men off the face and they lifted the switches off me. So they had to carry me out. I thought I'd have half a dozen broken ribs but I hadn't, as it happened. It had flattened me but there were only bruises. What I remember most about it was the night boss, Cyril Hughes, had no sympathy, because four of his men had had to leave the job to carry me out. That was the only thing he was worried about.'

Malc Beck who worked as an electrician at both Newdigate and Daw Mill was one of those who said he had never had an

Griff Clara colliery: taking part in a training exercise. (National Archives)

accident, then described one! 'I've not had any accidents. Well, I fell over just before I finished at Daw Mill and had thirteen stitches in my knee.'

When Malc was an apprentice he had to go round all the different shops on the bank. One of his favourites was the blacksmiths'. He told me, 'I used to love it in there. It's a real work of art, watching blacksmiths, proper blacksmiths bending metal and all that.

'But this particular day, I was in the carpenters' shop, and there was this little Geordie fellow. They needed some lagging boards, but they needed to be a certain length to go between the rings for packing. So the fork-lift truck drops these boards, and then he'd got to keep lifting them onto this huge bandsaw, and sawing them off at a certain length. Of course, familiarity breeds contempt. If you keep doing the same thing, you do start getting complacent. The next thing, he cut his thumb clean off. He went running into the painting end, shouting, "I've cut me thumb off!" The man there took him up to the medical centre, and when they get there, the nurse says, "Where's his thumb?" The painter says, "Well, it'll be down by the saw." The nurse says, "Go and fetch it, and they'll be able to sew it back on." So the painter ran back down back into the sawmill, but there is the sawmill cat licking its lips, with all blood round its mouth. The local carpentry cat had eaten his thumb. So they hadn't got a thumb to sew back on.'

Losing a finger or thumb seems to have been a regular occurrence in the pit. Malcolm told me of another incident. 'The worst one I've seen was a chap called Keith Gadsby, who was on this face. To cut a long story short, to help shove the face over, they come up with this idea of a hydraulic ram on the end of a box girder that had got another box girder inside it, with a series of holes drilled through the two. So once you'd shoved once, you could take the peg out, let it shove back and put a peg in again. Therefore it extended it.

'Well this particular day, they was ready to shove the front end over. Dalley were the charge hand on the face, and Keith Gadsby were at the front end. Everybody started shoving, so Keith does no more than takes the peg out. The girder slid in, then he's got to put the peg back in and try to line it up. So he done the most fatal thing in the world. He decides to use his finger to try to clear the hole out. Well, as he put his finger in, they started shoving again. The next thing he started screaming, "Stop shoving, stop shoving." There he was, screaming with his finger through the hole.

'So the deputy comes down. He says, "Oh, my god. I don't know how we're going to get him out of this." So he gets the old morphia out, choms it in his arm, squibs it. Then he says, "Right, get some pull lifts on the two girders now, pull them back together and see if we can line the two holes up and pull his finger out". They get these pull lifts on. They just started to pull and he started screaming again. The morphia hadn't done anything.

'It were making me feel bad. I thought, "I've got to go." You couldn't do anything for him and he was screaming. He was a mate of mine as well, the same age as me. So I went out of the pit. It was the end of the shift anyway. As I came out the pit, there was a doctor going down the pit to surgically remove his finger.

'Anyway, I went in the showers, and just as I was coming across the yard, there was Keith on a trambulance – a stretcher on wheels – and they'd cut his finger off. He says, "Malc, can you do me a favour? Can you take me car home?" So I went and got his keys and I drove his car home. The day after, he came over for his car. But they'd had to take his finger right off. They couldn't stick it back on.

'What had happened – we didn't know this at the time – there was a box girder inside a box girder, if the two holes had been lined up and his finger was through them both, when it moved it would have scissored it clean off. But it didn't. The box girder wasn't a brilliant fit, and his finger had gone trapped between the two girders, so there was no way it was going to come out. That was the worst thing I've seen down the pit.'

John Moffat told me of a man at Baddesley pit who almost lost his leg, but thanks to the help of the men with him, he did manage to avoid that fate. 'At Baddesley, a miner we called Bisto jumped on a belt that was a non man-riding belt and he went through a hole in the belt. It threw him over. His leg went over about twenty-odd rollers, and there was hardly anything left of it. But he survived and I think he's still knocking about. They even managed to save his leg. I think that was the care and attention of the people who were around him at the time that did that. There's nobody like pitmen when things like that happen. Nobody like them.'

However, some accidents result in a fatality. Peter Goodridge described two that he had experienced. 'There was a fitter who was actually doing something on top of the cage in the pit bottom. And the cage suddenly went up without a signal, and killed him. It virtually chopped him in half. On another occasion, the chief

Ansley Hall colliery: picking belts where stones etc were picked out from the coal. (National Archives)

engineer was on top of the headgear supervising the replacement of the winding wheels, when one of them swung round and knocked him off. He fell about a hundred feet below onto the concrete, so he was killed too.'

When Howard Baker was an overman at Binley, he and the manager, Mr Elter, were down the pit together. 'The manager and I went up this heading, and you're talking about 4 ft 9 ins high and 9 ft wide, supported on wooden props and a horizontal bar. We go up this heading, and when we gets to where the action is taking place, there's a guy there on the cutter, Ken Farr. He was just entering the cutter in. He was just starting to jib in. This machine had a long 6-ft jib on, high speed cutting chains on it. It was just at its most critical point where it was just starting to enter the coal. That's when it's going to vibrate if you haven't got the thing very firmly staked. Anyway, we goes up. The machine operator's on his knees, and the jibs going to swing round. I gets down by Ken and the manager comes to a position beside me.

'The jib's just entering the coal, and it jerked. The machine jumped. Ken Farr is trying to turn the thing off on the dead-man – press a button and then turn the handle off – and the jib moved. As I looked, our manager went straight into it. He was killed instantly. He didn't shout, there wasn't any blood or nothing. Just as Ken got the machine to stop, the final movement of the pick nicked his throat, and his head fell back. I went, "Bloody hell," and I turned away. That's when Ken gets his first view. He says, "Who the heck's that?" I said, "You've just killed the manager, Ken."'

Unlike many managers, Mr Elter had liked to spend a lot of time underground with the men. The subsequent inquiry established that he had always walked about with his hat on back to front and his cap lamp in his hand. That meant he always had a bit of loose cable, from the lamp to the battery on his belt. Howard went on, 'So when he went across to this machine with me, the machine just fractionally kicks, and there's no doubt – this was brought out at the inquest – what it did. It caught the cable of his lamp and whipped him in. It took the cable of his lamp and he went straight into the unit.'

Howard had a lot of time, a lot of respect, for the manager, telling me, 'The ironic part of it was that Mr Elter was a Luxembourger, and he'd fought in the Resistance. And as I understand it, he was awarded an honour for that. He finished the war, goes to university, comes into the mining industry as a graduate. He gets this job as the manager of Binley pit and then gets killed like that.'

A coalmine is inherently a dangerous place where accidents do occur. Even in an ultra-modern, computerised pit like Daw Mill, fatalities still happen. In a period of 2½ years, starting in 2006, Daw Mill suffered three fatalities. John Moffat, a NACODS official at Daw Mill, described them: 'Trevor Steeples, a deputy, he was gassed. Then the next one was Paul Hunt. That was at the top of the drift. He was nearly there. Another two yards and he would have been safe. The haulage was coming up the drift, and it stopped. The guy who was driving it put the power back on. It jerked violently and it threw Paul over. His head dropped into the rail, and he was killed. The third one was a fall underground. Because we went from coal tops to stone tops, the ribs were moving at the side. They were squeezing in. They were leaning at such an acute angle that either they were having to rib off or pin them back. This certain area had been ribbed off, and everybody thought it was safe. I'd actually been down there the morning before, and spoken to that guy, because he was a contractor. It was the first time I'd ever spoke to him in my life. The next time I seen him, he was dead.'

John has a very philosophical attitude to pit accidents, telling me, 'If the ducks line up, they will happen. There will always be accidents. People make accidents and the timings make accidents. As I say, when the ducks line up, it'll happen. Take one thing away, and it'd all collapse – the accident wouldn't happen. These fatalities occurred because everything lined up.'

Bill Joyce quoted an old colliers' philosophy about deaths in the pit that sent a shiver down my spine. He stated, 'At Coventry,

Daw Mill colliery: working the control point for the underground conveyor systems. (National Archives)

they used to reckon that a man was killed for every new district they dug. The old timers said that until a man was killed and the pit had had blood, the district would never be of benefit. It would always have troubles and problems until it'd had its blood. And then, when somebody was killed, they say, "It'll be all right now." And funnily enough, you would get a year or two year with no problems.'

Chapter 5

The Baddesley Pit Explosion

The explosion that took place at Baddesley colliery in 1882 cost the lives of 32 local miners. The mine was owned by William Stratford Dugdale, a wealthy landowner of nearby Merevale Hall, but it was run by his manager, John Parker.

By that time, mining was being carried out in a new district of the pit known as Deep Workings, which was reached via a one-in-three incline. The main problem in Deep Workings was water. The area was constantly flooding.

The mine owners had tried various ways to combat the water problem but none of them had been successful. Initially they removed the water with buckets and tubs, but this required a great amount of effort and time, and the water spilled from the tubs as they were taken up the steep incline. Next they tried installing a small pump in Deep Workings, powered by steam from a boiler on the surface. The steam had to be first piped down the shaft and then to the underground location. However, by the time the steam reached the underground pump, it was too weak to do the job of powering the pump.

Baddesley colliery. (National Archives)

What was needed was an underground boiler to provide the steam for the pump. The mining engineer, Frank Gillett, consulted a firm of mechanical engineers in Burton-upon-Trent, who recommended they install a pumping engine in the Deep Workings, which would need to stand on a brick platform with a brick archway constructed over it. The pump was installed at a point about 900 yards from the shaft bottom on 14th April 1882. The brick platform was built, as per Frank Gillett's instructions, and the new pumping engine placed on top of it. Because the roadway was only 5 ft high, the coal above the engine had to be excavated to make room for it. However, the roof – made of coal, it should be noted – was now only a few inches above the chimney of the new boiler. For some inexplicable reason, the second part of the instructions – that the new engine would need a brick arch over it – was never carried out.

Why the manager had failed to carry out the full instructions of the engineer was never discovered because John Parker was one of

Baddesley colliery: beam pump at Speedwell shaft. (National Archives)

those killed in the consequent disaster. We shall never know whether he was under instructions to hasten the installation, or whether it was on his own judgement that he made the disastrous decision. At the time, the pit was losing money and coal was only being turned on short-time working.

Gillett, who was not present for the installation, had also advised that the engine should only be in use for one day each week. This warning was also ignored, and the manager had the pump running continuously day and night, the heat, smoke, fumes and sparks from the engine being funnelled onto the coal roof a few inches above. Not surprisingly, it was soon noticed by the miners that the roof above the new engine was on fire. They doused the roof with buckets of water, and informed the manager. He decided to solve the problem by using a hose to spray water onto the roof over the engine, and this did turn the roof back from orange to black. However, although the roof was no longer glowing, it still continued to smoulder under the surface.

On the evening of Sunday, 30th April, part of the engine – a feed pipe to the boiler – broke, and the manager sent Joe Ball, an engine-wright, to assess what could be done. He could see that an immediate repair was not feasible, and the fire in the pumping engine was raked out.

By this time, the fire in the roof was glowing again, but nothing was done about this, either that night or on the Monday. Because the mine was on 'short time', there were only eight miners, plus a boy, on duty on the Sunday night shift. They were not digging coal, but had been sent in to do some repairs to the underground railway in Deep Workings. At 10 pm, Joe Day, the night-shift deputy, was going on duty as his father Charles Day was coming off. As Joe went down into the mine, he met thick black smoke. He reported this to his father, and the two men tried to get to the nine men working below. All the roadways were full of smoke – the only air was in the bottom 12 inches of the tunnel – and they were driven back.

Joe went up to the surface to raise the alarm, informing John Parker the manager, William Stratford Dugdale the owner and his agent John Pogmore. Meanwhile Charles Day had fetched three men working in another part of the pit, South Workings. Joe Day came back down with the manager and his son, plus three other men. The onsetter also remained at his post in the pit bottom. They constructed screens of wooden frames with brattice cloth stretched over them. They used these to try to push the smoke back down the incline, but a sudden rush of smoke defeated them.

John and Frank Pogmore went to fetch mining engineer Reuben Smallman from Chapel End. Smallman arrived in the pit at 2 am and took charge of the rescue efforts. Throughout the night and the next morning, news of the fire spread and more volunteers arrived to offer their help. The owner of the colliery arrived at 7.30 am to give his moral support to the rescuers in their attempts to reach the trapped men.

They were attempting to fix a permanent brattice screen across the tunnel, when at 8.30 am an explosion occurred. It was not a gas explosion, as Baddesley pit had never suffered problems with gas. This was a case of coal dust exploding and causing a sheet of flame to rush through the tunnel to where the rescuers were working, and most of them were badly burnt. All their lamps were blown out, leaving them in total blackness. Those less injured helped their more badly injured comrades back to the pit bottom, where the onsetter put them on the cage to be taken to the surface. All the men working on the screen except for two, Reuben Smallman and Henry Sanders, were to die of their injuries.

Reuben described the explosion as being like 'a whirlwind of fire, a whirlwind of small coal and dust, which lasted for about a minute.' Henry was to later describe his own injuries: 'The flesh of my hands hung in shreds, my face and head were charred and my legs burned even to my thighs.' Although Henry did survive, he had a breakdown and was unable at first to recognise his own village.

Another rescue party was sent down, this time to rescue the rescuers. Frederick Marsh, who had arrived from Hall End colliery to help, later described the injured men, 'Nearly all had their eyes burned quite out and their tongues were all shrivelled up.'

The dead and the injured were taken out of the pit, though some of these died of their injuries in the days that followed. In all, 23 men died as a result of the explosion, in addition to the eight men and the boy who were in Deep Workings when the fire broke out, making a total of 32 fatalities. Among the dead from the explosion were Mr Dugdale the mine owner, his agent John Pogmore and his son Frank, John Parker the manager, Joe Day the night-shift deputy and Joe Ball the engine-wright. The ages of the colliers who died in the explosion ranged from a 20-year-old to men in their fifties, many of them members of the same family, brothers or sons.

It was decided that it was now impossible to rescue the trapped men, who must be assumed to be dead. The cages were brought up to the top and the shafts were sealed with clay and mortar.

The tomb of John Pogmore and his son Frank in Merevale churchyard. Both were killed in the Baddesley pit disaster.

With the mine now airtight, the fire would slowly be quenched. The temperature inside the sealed pit was monitored, but it was November before the pit was deemed cool enough to re-open the seals. When the seal was broken, choke damp – carbon dioxide gas – poured out, but after a few hours this had diminished and the ventilation pumps were switched on. A day later, men were able to enter the mine. Their first gruesome task was to recover the bodies of eleven pit ponies.

Work in the South Side was able to resume, and for the first time in seven months, the Baddesley miners had work. The bodies of those who had died trapped in the Deep Workings were not recovered until April 1883, when three bodies were discovered almost a year after they had died. Another was found in November, and three more were recovered in July and August of 1884. Of the nine who died, overcome by smoke and fumes, trapped in Deep Workings, the youngest was 13-year-old Joe Scattergood, and oldest was William Day, aged 71. Joe Scattergood's body, along with that of Henry Radford, was never found. Deep Workings was permanently sealed and was never worked again.

The first body brought out of Deep Workings was identified, mainly through clothing, as John Ross and he was buried in Dordon. However, some time later, another body brought out was found to be that of John Ross, and it was decided that the first misidentified body was probably that of William Knight. Elizabeth Knight asked for her late husband's body to be exhumed and brought back from Dordon to his native Baxterley, but her request was refused. John Ross's widow Emma would have liked to have had a second funeral for her husband, this time with his genuine body, but her appeal for funds was turned down.

In February 1883, the heroism of the rescuers was officially recognised. Ten men were awarded medals. Four of them – Reuben Smallman, Arthur Stokes, Charles Day and Charles Chetwynd – received *The Albert Medal of the First Class*. Six others – Samuel Spruce, Frederick Marsh, Thomas Motram, William Morris, William Pickering and Joseph Chetwynd – were

The owner of Baddesley pit, William Stratford Dugdale, died in the disaster.
(National Archives)

awarded *The Albert Medal of the Second Class*. The relief committee also awarded specially-inscribed Bibles to the families of those who had lost their lives in the rescue, and to the surviving rescuers.

Of the total number of fatalities caused in the Baddesley pit disaster, 23 were married men, and 59 children lost their fathers. The whole community was devastated by the tragedy; 18 of the fatalities were from the villages of Baxterley and Baddesley Ensor, the rest coming from Grendon, Merevale, Atherstone and Dordon.

But, despite what had happened, the brothers, sons and grandsons of the men who had died continued to work as miners at Baddesley colliery. John Moffat worked at Baddesley pit himself from 1970 until it closed in 1989, as a collier, a shot-firer and a deputy. He told me, 'Baddesley colliery was an eerie place. Every one of the names of the men killed in the 1882 explosion is relevant today. The relatives, the same families, were still working at the pit when I was there.' That is, in my view, a fine testament to the mining spirit of North Warwickshire.

Note: An excellent book on the incident is *The Baddesley Pit Explosion 1882* by Celia E. Parton (Windmillfield Books 2009).

Chapter 6

Pit Humour

ike many people who work in difficult conditions – dealing with accidents and disasters – miners have their own sense of humour. Fire-fighters, paramedics, traffic police are the same. Having a laugh, making dark comments, winding up a friend or a gaffer can relieve the tension of the job. It is a necessary way of staying sane, dealing with intolerable events.

The humour of the pit can seem basic or even cruel, but it's the way men are, especially when they rely on each other for their safety, even for their lives. Malcolm Beck and Ev Emery, who worked together at Newdigate colliery, told me of one trick that was played on a man who prided himself on his physical strength. Malc said, 'One of my favourite stories is about Eli Eliott. He was a fit chap – there were some very fit chaps working at the pit. They'd got good bodies on them. There were four or five chaps working together, mixing this plaster up, putting these bags to finish this roadway off, then they plaster it, just to stop the air getting in so it doesn't catch fire. That's their job for the day. The deputy had been with them, and he

The pithead baths (opened in 1931) at Haunchwood colliery.
(National Archives)

said, "I've just got to go up further on. I'll come back to you in an hour."

'No sooner had the deputy gone, this Eli was stripped off. He was the sort of chap who, if you says to him, "I bet you can't do that," he'd have to do it. So one of the bloke says, "I bet Arthur here can take more stone dust bags on his chest than what you can." Eli says, "No he can't. We'll set it up then."

'They got Eli to lie down on his back, with Arthur lying head to head. All these bags of hardstop – plaster – are there. They said, "Right, we're going to start putting them on your chest." "Okay," Eli says. They put one on his chest and he never flinched. They put one on Arthur's chest, then another one on Eli's. It gets to about seven bags – and Eli couldn't see what was happening with Arthur – and of course by now they were pretending to put one on Arthur but they were really putting one on Eli. They'd got up to about thirty-five bags on him. They were piled up and it was putting the pressure on him – half a ton of bloody plaster on him.

'Of course, every time they were pretending to put one on Arthur, he were going, "Ugh!" Eli was proud that he was not making a noise. They kept putting another one on, and Eli's face was puffed out and red – busting with the pressure. They says, "That enough Eli? Cos Arthur's got thirty-six on him and you've got thirty-five?" Arthur had really only got about ten on. Eli grunts, "Put another one on!" They nearly killed him, honestly. They would have killed him if they'd carried on, but then they told him. He were a character, he were.'

Ev chipped in with another story about Eli. 'There was a belt man – Stevie – who got Eli with an oil-barrel. He said, "Eli, can you lift that oil barrel above your head?" Eli thought he was a body-builder, so he lifted this 25-litre barrel of oil up above his head, but what he didn't see was that when he went to pick it up, they jabbed a screwdriver in it. So he's standing there with the barrel over his head, and all the oil is coming down over him. And, until it starts coming off his helmet, he doesn't know.'

In those two stories, Eli was the butt of the joke, but he was always ready to join in with jokes on other people. Malc told me,

'Eli had split up with his wife, and although he was normally one for laughing and joking with the blokes, this day he sat there on his own, all subdued and not saying anything. People were worried that he was getting depressed.

'There was an electrician called Jess Farndon – known as the Bat, because he was supposed to be as blind as a bat – and this particular day he'd got an apprentice with him.

'They used to have jacky pits then to get onto this particular face. They were a hole in the ground, about 5-ft square and 20-ft deep, lined with steel and a ladder down it. To go onto the face from the tail gate, you'd have to go down this ladder and then onto the face – it was a queer set-up, really.

'Anyway Eli had a word with the Bat. He says, "What I want you to do is send your mate up just before snap time to come and fetch something out the tail gate." So sure enough, just before snap time, the Bat says, "Nip up to the tail gate. We want a new tannoy and there's one up there."

'So this apprentice starts going up this ladder, up this jacky pit. The next thing, something hits his head, and he turns round and there's Eli, hanging. What hit him was Eli's feet. He goes, "Oh my god. Eli's hung hisself!" He's panicking, as you can imagine, sheer panic. He runs down through the face, trying to get to the Bat. He's running and shouting, "Quick Bat. Come quick. Eli's hung hisself, he's hanging." The Bat says, "No, no, he wouldn't do that." "He has. I've seen him. He's hanging. His feet hit me on the head. You come with me."

'So, of course, they took him back up, by which time Eli had got hisself down from this noose he's made. The apprentice really thought Eli was dead. They had to show Eli to him, before he'd believe he was alive. He'd absolutely gone. That's pit humour!'

Bill Joyce remembered one nasty trick from his time at Coventry pit. 'One trick I remember. On the man-rider belt, you all piled on behind each other. In the low roof part, if the man in front didn't like them behind him, he'd pee on the belt, and because the belt sloped backwards, everyone got a share.'

John Moffat who worked at Baddesley colliery, then at Daw

Newdigate colliery social club. (National Archives)

Mill, told me, 'Very humorous, Baddesley was. The main man-rider was open, it was a rope man-rider with the old bell wires over the top. One train would be at the bottom and one would be at the top. And when they got to the mid-point they'd pass. This particular day somebody had took a rocking horse down. And as the overman was coming out, he was amazed to see this rocking horse going by him in the other direction. When it got to the bottom, somehow the rocking horse had disappeared.

'And then there was the trick that was done by me and my mate, Reuben. The pit was finishing, and there was a young fitter – Graham. Graham Sweet his name is. They were big families in Baddesley, the Sweets, the Peckovers, the Pethicks: all big mining families.

'Reuben was a good storyteller and a good winder-up. And he'd

Newdigate colliery: miners riding on the surface coal. (National Archives)

wound Graham up about the Onk. Now the Onk was the ghost that a lot of people had seen down Baddesley pit. And I'm not just on about people that you thought was a bit ga-ga. These were sensible people, people who you'd put your life in their hands. The ghost was called the Onk or sometimes Flat-Cap. A lot of people had seen him, including my dad, and he was a straightforward sort of bloke.

'The pit was finishing and we was salvaging this face. We knew exactly where Graham would be. We spoke to the deputy, Roger Wood, who was pre-shifting. And we knew Roger would be coming out with Graham.

'Reuben had got one of these old-man masks from Blackpool – it looks horrible with long grey hair. We got an old first-aid blanket and we cut it into a poncho. Reuben put the poncho on and the mask, and then we covered him from head to foot in stone-dust. To look at him, even the hackles on my neck were up. It was horrible. We'd told Roger about what we were going to do, so he was in on it. We asked the man-rider driver to slow it right down when he got to Five Stratford. As I say, these man-riders were all open.

'The train set away from the bottom, and it was probably about ten minutes before it gets to us. And as it come to us, it slowed down perfectly, absolutely perfectly. It was at a snail's pace as it started to climb the hill. I could see Roger sat there with his arms over the back, then Graham appears about two carriages back. He was sat the same. As he looks to his left, this figure just gently rises like it's floating. Because he was a big lad, Reuben, and he got up slowly. It looked really good, with the size of him. He just gently moved towards Graham and he touched him on the shoulder. We seen Graham turning and he went, "Roger, Roger, it's the Onk!" And as he said that, the train shot away. That threw him back. I could hear Roger saying, "What are you on about?" Roger was saying, "Look! Look!" And that was it. He was tumbling about in the back of the train.

'Now, we had to escape. We had to get up the belts, because he knew where we'd be, and if we weren't there, he'd guess we'd got something to do with it. So we jump on the belt, and we're running up it, trying to keep up, and I treads on the poncho. This stops Reuben and he goes over, and we're tumbling about on the belt. We gets up the top, out of breath. We'd left pasties on this transformer to warm up, and that's where we'd all meet up. That's where he'd expect us to be.

'We gets up there, out of breath. We just gets ourselves calmed down, and we could hear him coming round the corner, chuntering, "It's them pair, it's them pair. I know it is, I know it is." They come up and Roger says, "He reckons he's seen the Onk." I says, "What are you on about?" Roger says, "He's seen the Onk. He says it's just touched him." Graham says, "It's you two, I'm telling you." I says, "What are you on about? We've been here. We've done our inspections, we've come back up, and we've sat here for an hour." He says, "I know it's you two," and he started searching. But he never found nothing. Until this day, he still believes it was the Onk.'

Another example of miners' humour was connected to a man they called Ferret. John Moffat told me, 'Ferret was one of two brothers, the Wilkins. They used to have a little Jack Russell that they used to take up the pub at Baxterley. I think it was called the Lion – it's shut now. There was a bench outside, and they used to sit the dog on the bench, and put a Woodbine in its mouth so that anybody going by thought the dog was smoking.

'In the pub, the dartboard had a length of belting on the floor, pit belting. The deputy manager used to drink in there, Webster he was called. And I heard that the Ferret was in one night, and his dog's lying in front of the dartboard, on the belt. The deputy manager walks in and he kicks the dog, and he says, "Get off the belt. You know the rules about illegal man-riding!"'

Malc Beck also mentioned a miner's revenge on the overman. ''Arry 'All hated this particular overman, because he were old-school. He looked back to the old days where if you wanted to work the weekend, you used to have to give the overman some tobacco or snuff. A bribe. He used to talk to people like it were them days. He would walk up to you and say, "Got any snuff?"

"No." "Why not? Got any bacca then?" He used to sort of demand it off you.

'This overman had always got a stick with him, his overman's stick. This day, he decided to go in this heading, and he decided not to take his stick in with him. Anyway he goes in the heading, leaving his stick, and it were obvious it were his stick with the ball on the top. And this contractor came and said, "That's the overman's stick, ain't it?" I said, "Yeah." "Right, I'll show him." So he does no more, he gets a bloody hacksaw out and saws it so there's just the top ball and about a foot of stick. Then he shoved it in the ground, so it looked like he'd buried this stick right up to the top. Of course, the overman comes up and he says, "Where's my stick? I left it there." Then he spots it and, thinking it's buried, he says, "Who's put that there?" He went to tug it out, and because it was only a foot long he went flying backwards. Oh bloody hell fire, it was that funny. Some of the cracks they used to get up to was hilarious.'

It wasn't just the officials that the miners liked to wind up. Malcolm Beck told me of one occasion when he and an apprentice were breaking the rules by riding out on the belt. 'This particular day we was down the pit, and I'd got an apprentice with me, Cade Bend his name was. We was riding up the main on number four belt. We didn't know that the under-manager Colin Shillitoe and the manager Tom Flemming were walking up the road. Well, you weren't supposed to ride this belt. I come underneath the rip, and there's Colin Shillitoe and the manager walking up. The manager had a brass peck – his stick – and a beige coat on, that was a sign of management. I couldn't get off the belt, and I was riding past.

'The manager shouts, "Get off the belt!" I jumped off. At which point my apprentice comes riding through. "And you get off as well!" The manager came walking up with this brass peck, with Colin next to him. He says, "What d'you think you're doing?" He lifts his stick up and he points at Colin Shillitoe, and he says to me, "Come and see Mr Shillitoe in the morning before you go down the pit. And your mate." He waltzed off, and I thought, "I can't believe I've done this." The apprentice wanted to know what'd happen and I said, "Well, we're gonna get fined."

Sure enough, the next morning we went into the electric shop and I says to Alan Morris, the chargehand, "I can't go down the pit straightaway. I've got to see Colin Shillitoe." "Why's that?" he says. "He caught me on the belt." "Silly bugger. Fancy getting caught …" I waited there and I see the little pit van come. I see him get out and go in his office. I gave him five minutes and said, "I'll go in first." When I went in, he sighs, "Oh Malcolm. Fancy letting the manager catch you on the belt. I've got to fine you, you know that, don't you?" He opens his drawer and looks at the list of all the previous people who've been fined. "Right," he says. "I'm going to fine you three pound, is that all right?" I says, "Yes, Mr Shillitoe," as if I could argue. He says, "Here y'are. Sign there." As I went to walk out the office, he says, "Send your mate up." Then as I was going out, he says, "Malcolm, it's only the price of a drink, ain't it?"

'I went down to the shop and of course Cade was stood by the door. He says, "What did you get? What did you get?" To wind him up, I said "A £10 fine." He shouts, "Oh no! I owe me mother ten quid this week. I won't have no money at all. I'm never going down the pit with you again." I said, "Well, you better go up there." Of course he went waltzing in, and Colin Shillitoe must have said, "Look, I've fined your mate three quid, so it's just £1.50 for you." So when Cade come back out, he says to me, "You bastard!"'

At the beginning of this chapter I did say that pit humour could be very earthy, very down to earth. Anyone of a sensitive nature might be best advised to go straight to the beginning of the next chapter. For those of you still left, here are Malc and Ev's memories of their colleague Jeff Parsons' amazing anatomy.

'Jeff Parsons had got a hole in the end of his penis. I'd never seen anything like it before. He were born with it. This was a hole he could put a padlock through! He could hang a padlock or a Davy lamp off the end of his penis. It weren't painful.

'One day a miner named Mo turned round to him and he says,

A group of miners in a gate at Newdigate colliery. (National Archives)

"Jeff, there's a new bloke in the ambulance room. Do you want to do something with the hole in your penis?" So he gets a six-inch nail, shoves it through, he gets a bit of tomato sauce, and squibs it over it. He went down to this surgery with it covered up with his hands. He walks in and this young ambulance bloke says, "What have you done then?" Jeff says, "Well I've had a bit of an accident with a nail." He says, "Have you. Come on, you haven't got anything I haven't seen before. Let's have a look." Of course, Jeff moves his hand away, and there's this 6-inch nail straight through. "How the bleeding hell have you done that?" You can imagine, can't you, the look on this bloke's face! He was such a card, Jeff.

'If we had somebody who didn't know about it – we had lots of fitters and electricians come down the pit at Newdigate – Jeff used to say, "Pass me a lock." We used to give him a lock, and he'd put the hasp through. He'd just line it up so it looked like it were locked. And if there were a new bloke hadn't seen it, you'd set it up for him. You'd say, "Are you out tonight then, Jeff?" He'd say, "Well I'm going out but I shan't be enjoying myself. The missus has put the lock on again." Well, of course, the new bloke who didn't know anything about it would say, "What you on about? Put the lock on?" He'd say, "Oh, didn't you know? The missus makes sure I don't play with other women when I go out." "What d'you mean?" "Well I'll show you." At which point, he'd drop his penis out, and the bloke would go, "Oh my god!" It was brilliant to look at the bloke's face when he saw that padlock.'

On Malc's last shift at Newdigate, he decided to turn the joke on Jeff. 'We were waiting for the man-rider to come up, and Jeff Parsons was there. There was this trainee under-manager stood on the corner. So I says, "Ay up Jeff, I bet he hasn't seen the crack with the lock, has he?" He says, "No. Give us your lock." So I got my lock out and I undone it, Jeff slips it on. He's just lining it up so it looks like it's locked, at which point I leaned over and snapped it shut, then threw the keys down the road. "What the bleeding hell are you doing?" he's going on. Well, I'm laughing my socks off. Jeff's running down the road, still wearing this lock, to look for these keys. I wished he hadn't found them – it would have made my day for him to have to get the lock cut off – but there were too many keys on the bunch, so he found the bloody things.'

Pit humour at its most earthy!

Chapter 7

Strikes

Although some newspapers and certain politicians like to allege that miners were always out on strike, it should be remembered that there were no national miners' strikes between 1926 and 1972. That is 46 years. Hardly a legacy of militancy.

By 1972, the wages of the miners had fallen behind many other working groups, and those who knew of their working conditions were not surprised when they voted for a national strike.

The Ted Heath government resisted the miners' wage claim, and in January 1972 the miners came out on strike. Miners supported the strike overwhelmingly, and they had a lot of public support. Although all the pits stopped work, the miners knew that the way to win quickly was to stop the supply of coal to the power stations.

By the beginning of February, the only coke depot still working was at Saltley in Birmingham. Saltley was dispatching 700 lorries a day loaded with coke, and the Warwickshire miners decided to picket the place. One of them was Bill Joyce from Coventry pit. On his first visit, he was somewhat surprised to be accused by the police of not being a miner. Bill told me, 'I was on the front gate at Keresley, and our union rep asked me if I'd go over to Birmingham to picket at Saltley. I got off the bus, put me bag down, and went to join the picket line. A lorry was coming up, and I went to join the line to ask him to stop.

'The next second, I'd got a hand on my shoulder. "I want you!" The police had got me. And that was my first picket. I was in there all day – they kept moving us about from police station to police station so nobody knew where we were. What amused me, when this inspector cautioned me, he said, "What university are you from? We know all about you. We've been told you were coming to organise." I said, "Do I look university?" He says, "Yes. Which one is it?" I suppose there must have been students coming over, sympathisers, to help the miners. I'd been up in my garden shed, and I said to the inspector, "Look here," and I showed him I'd got nails and all sorts in my pocket. He still didn't believe me, and he actually come to my house to see, to check if I was a miner!'

Bill went on, 'It was a marvellous place, Saltley, really marvellous. We were a bit short at first, and there were about ten police for every picket. The police were back-heeling us and kicking, truncheons and elbows. I said, "Well, give 'em time. It's a bit early, Inspector. Some of these people have got to come a long way, you know. We've been up since three, you know." He just laughed at me and said, "You won't win."

'About half an hour later, three coaches full of miners arrived. They'd come from Scotland. Three coaches of 'em. One man jumped out, and he started playing the bagpipes. The Scottish miners had come to join us on the picket line. Then two more coaches come by.' Miners began arriving from all over the country to join what became known as the Battle of Saltley Gates. Bill told me that the local people were brilliant. 'They were bringing us sandwiches and tea in flasks. They were great. And the Birmingham people would put up two or three pickets to sleep in their houses.'

It wasn't just miners who joined the picket line. Bill recalled, 'A chap come up to us and asked me what it was like. He was one of the stewards from the local factories. He says, "We've had a talk with our unions, and we'll be here, as well. Expect us in about an hour." The police had sealed all the streets off. But he said, "Don't worry. We're local. We know ways to get here. There'll be another three or four hundred down just now."

'Well, when they came, it absolutely whelmed the place out. Nobody could move. Everything was shut when these people from the factories come out. They were brilliant. This inspector – the one that'd said, "You won't win" – he were there, shouting, "Shut it down. Shut it down." And they did, they shut the gates.' The closing of Saltley Coke Depot proved crucial and as power cuts occurred throughout the country, the government was forced to make a deal with the miners.

John Moffat was still an apprentice at the time, and apprentices were not allowed out on strike. He said, 'In the '72 and '74 strikes we were classed as apprentices then. We actually worked. We were down the plant, cleaning up down the washroom. And the manager told us to go and get some coal, take it down to the pickets and make sure they're all right. He looked after them with food and a bottle to keep them warm. He used to send coal down for the braziers. That was our job in the morning, to make sure they'd got enough supplies.'

Malc Beck was also an apprentice at the time. 'Yes I was there in 1972 and '74. I was an apprentice in both of them, because I started in 1970. The apprentices had to work. I can remember the first one. We just turned up at the pit and we couldn't go down, so we just run riot on the bank. I can remember in the '72 strike, all of a sudden this articulated lorry pulls in with a load of hardstop. Hardstop was a plaster that they used down the pit, a sealant. How the lorry got past them on the gate I don't know. This lorry pulled in, and of course there was nobody to unload it. So the next thing, somebody out the offices turns round to us apprentices and said, "Right, unload that lorry." So we jumps up and starts chucking these bags off the lorry. Next thing, three or four of the pickets come down, saying, "Get that bastard stuff back on there." Well, the bags went back on twice as quick as they'd come off, and the lorry went off as full as when it came in. "You do not do that," they said to us. We didn't know any better, we was only doing as we was told.'

Ev Emery commented, 'There was a lot of sympathy in the '72 and '74 strikes. The miners were underpaid in them days. I was at Newdigate in the '72 strike, and there were two local hospitals – the George Elliot was one and there was another one somewhere – where we let them have coal for the heating. And they got a ticket saying that they had to have coal. They used to come up to the picket line and say, "Sorry lads but we've got to get some coal for the hospital," and we said, "No problem." They used to bring a couple of bags out, one for themselves and one for the pickets' brazier. The pickets always had a brazier on the pit gates.'

The year-long strike of 1984–5 proved rather different. This was not about pay; it was to maintain a UK coal industry, to stop the government closing down the pits. The prime minister by then was Margaret Thatcher, and she was determined to defeat the National Union of Miners. For one thing, they had brought down the Ted Heath government ten years earlier. She also had a plan to reduce the coal industry to a small number of mines, which could then be privatised.

She prepared well, building up stocks of coal at the power stations and then provoking the miners into coming out on strike in the spring. A miners' strike always worked best in the winter. She did this by closing down Corton Wood pit in South Yorkshire, in the heart of Arthur Scargill's home area. Yorkshire came out on strike, as did Scotland, Kent, South Wales, North Derbyshire, Durham and Northumbia.

In Warwickshire the miners at Coventry came out to support the union. Bill Joyce said, 'In the '84 strike, I'd just finished, retired, but we used to go up and support the lads on the picket line. It was surprising the amount of women who came from different places, bringing bits of food up, and flasks of tea. It was good.'

Coventry colliery was behind the strike but at other Warwickshire pits, the feeling was less supportive. Malcolm Beck, who by that time was at Daw Mill, explained, 'There was a few pits out, and I went to work this day and everybody was milling about in the foyer. We didn't know what to do. To be honest, a lot of us were teetering on coming out on strike. I stood there with

Coventry colliery. (National Archives)

this Joe Starkey, and I says, "I don't know what to do, Joe." He said, "I tell you what, I'm going back home."

'And he walked out the foyer door – he'd only been gone about three or four minutes – and he come back in. He says, "I'm not going home – I'm working." I turned round and I says, "What are you on about?" He says, "I've just gone to my car now, and I was quite sympathetic with the pickets on the gate, but then one of them shouted, 'We've got you now, you bastards. You won't work for the next twelve months.'" He says, "Nobody's telling me when I'm gonna work and when I'm not gonna work. So I'm working." And, with that, quite a few men says, "If that's how they're thinking, then I'm working an' all. We're not being told what to do."'

John Moffat described what happened at Baddesley. 'We were expecting the pickets all week. We were on nights, and on the Thursday night I went to work and as I pulled into the pit yard, a body shot across my bonnet. He said, "Yorkshire picket, Yorkshire lads. Are you working tonight?" And then a female voice from the right come, "And lasses!" They'd even brought their women with them. The manager pulled us all back to the canteen, and he had words with them, telling them to get off the premises.

'Well, next morning, when he asked us to come back up, there was police everywhere. That's how it was. The whole of the surrounding areas was fenced off. Baddesley and Daw Mill were not particularly good places to get to, because they're in country lanes. Daw Mill is in a steep incline, so as you approach it, when the trees are up, you wouldn't even know it was there. And Baddesley was off the main road – the A5 – and you wouldn't even know that was there until you got to it.'

Like a lot of miners who decided to work instead of joining the

Daw Mill colliery. (National Archives)

miners on strike, Malcolm blamed the lack of a national ballot. 'Arthur Scargill didn't want the vote. He ballsed it up, really. If they'd have gone for the vote when they should have done, everybody would have been out. But when they didn't want the vote, and they was gonna tell you we're going on strike, that was it.'

John Moffat agreed. 'We hadn't had a national ballot, and as far as we were concerned, we understood his issues, we knew what was going to happen, and if they'd have given us a national ballot, we'd have all been on the same wavelength and I'm sure everybody would have been out. There was a few at Baddesley went out for a start, but then they returned. They'd got no choice really because they were just losing money. But I think it was a sad state of affairs, especially when they went back. It was a crying shame. A year out for nothing, because it was the ordinary Joe who suffered, to be honest, and their families. It caused a lot of grief.'

However, speaking to the miners who supported the strike, they made the point that the idea of a national ballot had been destroyed some years earlier when the NUM balloted in 1976 against a bonus scheme that the Coal Board wanted to bring in. Although the NUM won the ballot, the courts later ruled that those areas that wished to use the bonus scheme could do so, despite the national ballot.

One striking miner told me, 'The scabs were like sheep, bleating "baa-lot, baa-lot". Yorkshire miners, Welsh miners, Kent miners, miners in the north-east were all saying, "You're not stabbing us in the back with a national ballot again. We know what the scabs want to do. If we have a ballot and it goes for a strike we know what they'll do, they'll carry on working." A national ballot wouldn't have made any difference; that was proved in 1976. We knew the scabs would not abide by the result of a national ballot if it went against them. Anyway, real miners would never cross a picket line – no trade union man would. It's against everything we believe in.'

Malcolm Beck commented, 'We went through the picket line

one day on about fifteen buses. This particular day, they all lined up on the main road, in a convoy, and they all went in through the gates like a bat out of hell. There were hundreds of pickets there. It was a terrible time.' Ev Emery added, 'My wife – she was still alive then – she had a relation who was well up in the police force, and he said that word had come down from higher authorities that as long as Daw Mill men wanted to work, they would get through. No matter how many police it took. The local firm – Wainfleet – they had a lot of buses, and the bus drivers were sympathising with the strikers and didn't want to go through the gates. They were going to stop outside the gates with the men having to walk through the pickets. But the Wainfleet's gaffer said, "Daw Mill pays my wages and it keeps my buses going." The drivers were told they had to drive through.'

The pickets had very little trouble with the local police, but the police who were brought in from other areas, particularly the Met, were a different matter. Malcolm Beck commented, 'The Met police were brought in for a purpose. The canteen were full of them.'

Not all the working miners were happy with the behaviour of the police brought in to control the pickets. One miner told me, 'There was a load of Welsh pickets across the road at our pit, and there was a big sergeant from the Met stood there, a big strapping bloke with a helmet on and a big black coat. An apple core come over and it hit the sergeant on the side of the helmet. He said, "I want one of them now!" And they pulled this youth out, dragged him through the hedge – they didn't know whether it was him or not – and they was just kicking the shit out of him. One of the working miners called out, "Is there any need for that?" This big copper says, "Do you want to be the next one?" I just walked off. They were the Met, not local police, and they were out of control.'

Arthur Scargill may have been a bête noir – a hate figure – to some tabloid newspapers and to many miners who worked during the strike, but not to all mining officials. Howard Baker, who rose through the ranks to become a deputy manager, told me, 'Arthur Scargill? When I was out on courses, I met colliery managers from

Yorkshire, who invariably said that, when he had been into their office on the odd occasion over a dispute, it was always conducted fairly. There was never any wrong with Arthur Scargill when they had dealings with him. That's what I heard about him.'

Ken Lewis, a miner at Coventry colliery for nineteen years, put his thoughts into a powerful poem he called *The Strike of 84:*

> *We were called on to strike in March eighty-four*
> *All thinking it wouldn't take long*
> *For we toppled the Tories on our last big strike*
> *Our faith in our Union was strong.*
>
> *But Maggie had planned her moves for six years*
> *To bring down the miners' big force*
> *Just imagine facing the awesome sight*
> *Of a club-swinging thug on a horse.*
>
> *The gallant police would soon bring us down*
> *The army men helped swell their ranks*
> *Between dogs and horses, helmets and shields,*
> *It's a wonder they didn't bring in tanks.*
>
> *I didn't take part in all of that strife*
> *Just to picket each day was a fraction*
> *Of some of the things the youths had to do*
> *To be in the front line of the action.*
>
> *They put us old codgers to picket the gates*
> *To stop lorries, the front gate and back*
> *But if you just once stepped out of line*
> *You'd be faced with the threat of the sack.*
>
> *Watch what you're saying, or out you will go,*
> *Gone is your job and your pension.*
> *All them years lost that you slaved down the pit*
> *Was too frightening even to mention.*

Two of my mates that stood at them gates
Retired the same time as me
They both passed away a few months ago
At the Golden Gates now they stand free.

God bless them both and keep them safe
They were both true Union men
When will we ever again see their likes?
No doubt we will meet them again.

It was very sad to see your old mates,
Mates that you'd worked with for years,
Passing the picket line despite your pleas
Your arguments fell on deaf ears.

The Manager stopped by the pickets one day.
He spoke to me in gruff tone,
"What have you gained in this strike, boyo lad?"
I answered him, "Frankly, two stone."

The twenty-six strike was stuck in our minds:
We had listened to all the tales.
After watching two thirds of our workforce go back
I wished I was back home in Wales.

We went back to work, the strike at an end,
No guts left for work, only tears.
I wanted to sell my job, I'd had enough.
We'd turned back the clock forty years.

So on that morn with banners held high,
Although our ranks were quite thin.
Our thoughts were with the sacked men left behind
With the promise to fight from within.

Ken Lewis (fourth from left) picketing at Coventry pit, 1984.

What of the sacked men? Their jobs are now gone.
They had struggled and landed in prison.
God help the future of our men in the pits
With UDM and Thatcherism.

We can all see now Arthur's words were true,
For a lot of our pits are no more.
We've seen enough strife to last us our life,
We will never forget eighty-four.

No other union ever fought so hard,
We fought for our jobs and our right.
Maggie thanked old McGregor for closing our pits
By bestowing the honour of Knight.

They called him the axeman, now he's a Sir,
The next thing she'll make him a martyr.
One thing I thank, there's no room for Sir Yank
In the NUM court of King Arthur.

Chapter 8

Howard and the Smokers

When **Howard Baker went to** Binley colliery as a young over-man, he met an unusual situation. Binley was a smoking pit! The miners there routinely ignored the ban on smoking underground. This ban was brought in for all pits in 1947, but ten years later, the ban was still being ignored at Binley.

Howard explained, 'Binley was a pit where CH4 – methane gas – was virtually unheard of. And because of this, they used to smoke underground. Originally, it was a Scott's-owned colliery and they were allowed to get away with it, but in 1947 the industry was nationalised, and they brought in an overall no-smoking ban. However, at Binley nobody ever stamped it out. And I was led to believe that even if they did get caught, it was just half-a-dollar fine and a smack on the hand. And that was about it.

'I first heard about the problem when I was working at Kingsbury and when I was doing my training. People from other pits who had been to Binley underground, they used to notice tobacco smoke. Well, we were all horrified, of course. Elsewhere in the county, it was absolutely unheard of.

Binley colliery. (National Archives/Mr D. Slaney)

'Then in 1957 I went to Binley as an overman. One thing I wasn't going to tolerate was any smoking. But a lot of the senior people at Binley must have had something wrong with their sense of smell, because when I used to say, "I can smell smoke," they'd say, "Oh no, I can't smell anything." I wasn't the only young official there, there were four of five of us, and we all decided we weren't going to tolerate it.

'We started to go round different areas at different times, so that they didn't know we were coming. What we found, once some of the officials – and some of the men – knew that we weren't going to tolerate it, they used to give us bits of information. They would not tell you who was doing the smoking, but they would say, "If you go and look in this or that place, you might find cigarettes or matches." We started to do that with a fair amount of success.

'At the same time, the management had belatedly decided to be strict, and they started to take people to court. We used to go down to Rugby court to charge the people with having matches and cigarettes down the pit. You could be in a lot of trouble if you smoked down the pit – and the NUM was against it as much as the management – but at Binley, because of its history, it had always been a smoking pit up to the time it was nationalised, and it had carried on. Originally, if they were caught it was just a fine. But in the end, the Coal Board legal department decided that it was such a serious offence – they must have had some communications at the upper levels – that they decided any smoking offence would go to court. We had a couple or three go to court. Smoking is an offence under the Coal Mines Act.

'Anyway, we got a bit of expertise at finding out where people used to hide their cigarettes and matches. One regular place was to put them inside a contraceptive inside a water bottle. Some used to put them inside a powder can of all places! Other people would have something sewn under their shirt collar or in their shorts, where they could hide a couple of matches and a couple of fags. And some people used to hide them on the top of the girders, in the flange of a girder. So when we were examining the pit, as we had to, we were going along feeling over the girders.

'And in the end, after one or two court cases, we about knocked it on the head. You had to be careful, though. I were walking down a roadway at the end of a shift with one of the younger deputies, and he put his coat on. He walked out with me, and he put his hands in his pocket and says, "Oh bloody hell." He didn't smoke, but in his pocket was a packet of Senior Service. One of the smokers had put them in there. So you had to be very aware.'

The competition between on one side Howard and those trying to stamp out the dangerous habit and on the other side the smokers almost became a game, a contest. Howard recalled, 'The best story about the smoking happened when I went up this road one day, up the return airway. And I could smell lots of smoke coming down. They were all smoking.

'I knew that the face had had a reasonable day, and that they'd all be done at a reasonable time. I goes under the road head onto the face. There they are, all sat down in the sticks, about five or six yards apart. I knew who the smokers were, and I thought I'd head down the coal face. And as I goes down, I can see a glow. I got down to these two characters who I knew were two of the worst culprits. I said, "Okay lads, we're gonna have a search."

'The first thing we had to do was invite them to search us. They said, "Well, we're not really bothered about searching you, gaffer, are we?" I said, "Well, it's your option." They said, "We can help you though. We'll help you find whatever you're after." I thought, "I reckon I've lost this one."

'Anyway, I searched their shirts and their shorts, and they said, "Have a look in our boots." Nothing in there. "How about our powder can, d'you want to look in there? Water bottle?" We went all through the gamut of places. I went and searched the conveyor in case they'd flicked their fag end or the match down there. I went over the conveyor into the gob, in case they'd flicked them in there. Nothing.

'I came back to them and I said, "Okay, you two, that's it. I haven't caught you. But I hope you know that was a near miss. Next time I might be a shade more lucky." They said, "Ah, okay, we understand that." That was it. Off I went. The following morning, I'm down at the meeting station, and all the guys come up. And this one, Yorkie Howard, says, "You nearly had us, you know, yesterday. That was a near squeak. I was as sick as a dog when I got home and had me dinner." They'd only had to swallow their cigarettes and matches! But they said that was it. They were packing it in.

'Then we caught an under official, a deputy, who smoked underground. We knew he'd been smoking – we'd had a bit of inside information. We found the evidence when he was off work one day. It was in the pit holidays and he was off that day, and we was searching round the girders, and we found some cigarettes and this box of matches with a piece of paper in it. The smokers used to put a piece of paper in the matchbox so the matches wouldn't rattle. But he'd torn the corner of a page off his notebook with his writing on it. And this guy had excellent handwriting – his writing was a picture. And as soon as we saw this slip of paper and the writing on it, we knew it was him.

'So we went out the pit and saw the under-manager and he said,

"Well, I don't know what to do about that. I'd better ring the manager." We went over to see the manager, and he said, "The best thing you can do for a start is to open his locker and see if his notebook's in his overall pocket." And it was, with the corner torn off. That case then went up the Coal Board legal department, and they decided that they would prosecute it, because it was a deputy, and they wanted to stamp the smoking out. The union – NACODS – decided, as was their right, to fight the case, because it was purely circumstantial. That went to Warwick Assizes, where it was proved in the Coal Board's favour, and the man was sacked. Obviously, it was a hell of a blow to the man concerned.

'One thing that did make me laugh once was when I was searching these other two guys. When I'd finished searching, I says

Haunchwood miners relaxing after their shift.

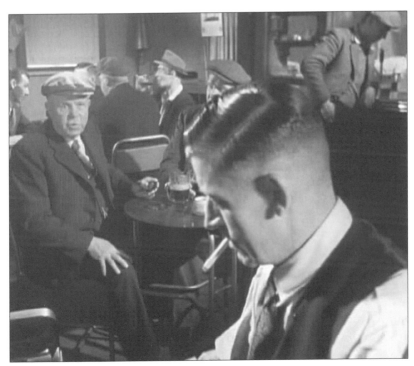

"Okay, that's it lads." One of these lads says to me, "I can show you somewhere where you haven't looked." You can guess what he did then. He dropped his shorts and bent over.'

Eventually the practice of turning a blind eye to the smokers was wiped out and Binley kept to the universal rule of not allowing any miner to smoke or to take matches underground. The game was over. Howard Baker and the younger officials had won, and the smokers had lost.

Chapter 9

Ponies, Mice and Flies

Although few of the Warwickshire miners I spoke to had ever worked with ponies down the pit, one or two of them could remember them. John Moffat told me, 'Before I came to Baddesley colliery, there were ponies there, but none in my day. However, my dad moved down to Warwickshire from Scotland in the 1960s and my family lived at Kingsbury, in the pit yard. They were terraced houses, pit houses – two rows with a street down the middle – and the back of the houses led onto a field. We were more or less in the middle of Kingsbury pit yard. And I remember, when I was a kid, seeing all the ponies coming into the field in the summer shutdown, and then kicking up when they tried to get them back down the pit. I know the stores and everything were still in Baddesley pit when I went there, but the ponies had gone.

Howard Baker can remember ponies being at Kingsbury pit, though. 'At Kingsbury we must have had thirty or forty ponies. We worked in two seams at Kingsbury: the Seven Foot and the Bench. I suppose the difference in level was about forty yards. So there was Seven Foot shaft and Bench shaft – different shafts – so

Pit ponies at Amington colliery.

the horses weren't interchangeable. They had to have stables in the Seven Foot and stables in the Bench.

'Have you heard stories about horses on the conveyor belt? Where the ground had shoved in a bit at the side, and where the horse was supposed to go up alongside the conveyer, sometimes when the road encroached, you couldn't get the horse past on the tracks. So they'd take the tackle up so far, offload it, put the horse on the belt, and take the horse round on the conveyer.

'The ponies could always find their way out at the end of a shift. They always let the horse go on his own, and he'd find his own way to the stables in the dark. Ponies could do that. And they also had ponies at North Warwickshire colliery – Pooley Hall, Amington and Alvecote pits. They were all separate pits until they

*Typical miners' cottages – these belonged to Ansley Hall colliery.
(National Archives)*

Miners' houses at the Shortwoods, Dordon colliery. (National Archives)

Alf King, with a pit pony in the late 1930s.

In the locker room at Pooley Hall colliery. (National Archives)

joined together and were called North Warwickshire colliery. They definitely had ponies there.'

Ev Emery recalled, 'When I done my training at Wood End, there were thirteen pits in Warwickshire, but only one that still had ponies. And because there was still ponies at Pooley Hall pit, we still had to learn pony haulage. The ponies we trained with didn't go down the pit, but they'd made a mock-up place on the bank. You had to hook the pony up and go through. We were young lads, but there were people there who had been with ponies all their life. They loved them ponies. We had to groom the pony, and put the harness on. The trainer said, "This pony, if you've got an apple or orange in your pocket, watch him." When you put the harness on, he'd have the apple or orange out your pocket.

'To make it dark, because you got half a pit lamp on, they'd dug a trench, put rings up and filled it in. And they put a bend in it and air doors, so it were dark. And that pony, he'd wait till you got through the air doors and then he'd fart. He done it regular. I'll tell you what, the pony got used to us kids. We were just kids, weren't we. And another thing, when you got to the end of the road, if that pony wanted a drink, he went for a drink. It didn't matter if there was ten of you, he went for a drink when he wanted one.'

When Peter Goodridge was at Wood End in 1951, there was just one pony left – and it had retired. 'While I was at Wood End, the superintendent wanted to know if anyone had worked on a farm. Well of course I'd worked on the poultry farm, so I put my hand up, not being old enough to realise that you don't volunteer for anything if you don't know what it's about. Apparently, Birch Coppice's last pit pony had come up and retired, and he was stabled at Wood End. So I got the job of taking him for a walk, exercising him for about an hour every morning.'

Although the ponies had all but disappeared, there was other livestock to look out for. Peter informed me, 'No account of coalmining would be complete without a mention of our constant underground companions: the mice. One of the first things you learn – usually the hard way – was to be careful where you put your snap. The only sure safeguard was to have a metal snap tin, but most miners took theirs down the pit simply wrapped in newspaper. A fairly sure way was to hang your snap from the roof using a length of detonator wire. This was very thin plastic-covered wire attached to the detonators used for shot firing. String was no good – mice can climb down string. It was very annoying at snap time to find a hole in the middle of your sandwiches.

'We used to put some bread into a tub or mine car, and rear a plank up against it. The mice would climb up the plank, and fall down into the tub to get the bread. Then we would run water into the tub and drown the little bleeders. It may seem cruel, but they really were an utter menace. You could be sitting in the gate, and you would feel one up your trouser leg! Luckily, it couldn't get past your knee because of your kneepad straps, but still it wasn't very nice.'

Sometimes, a young miner would not have the knowledge that the older miners had accumulated. Malcolm Beck recalled, 'I hadn't been down the pit long, and I was with Horace Pitchford this particular day. We was bolting some panels up round this corner, a new bank of panels. I didn't know what the crack was, and there was another bank of panels just round the corner. We stopped at this first bank of panels, I took my coat off and hung it on the socket of the panel. I'd got my snap – about eight cheese and pickle sandwiches. I was really looking forward to them, because as a young lad, you can eat like there's no tomorrow. They were just in bags, and I'd put them on top of this panel.

'Anyway, we were working round the corner until snap time come at a quart to ten. Horace says, "We'll have our snap now." Of course, he'd hung his up on a piece of string like you're supposed to do. He says, "Where's your snap?" I says, "Well, I've left it on the panels round the corner." He looked at me as if to say this is a learning curve. He says, "You better go and get it then." So I walked round the corner. Well, you've never seen so many mice – all going through my snap. There was tunnels through the sandwiches, and they were scattered everywhere. And I was starving an' all. I thought, "I can't believe this." So I never had nothing to eat that day. But it teaches you a lesson. You do not put your snap down where they can get to it. Even if you tied it up and hung it up, you'd see 'em coming down the string.'

Malcolm's friend Ev intervened to say, 'I've still got my old pit tin, my snap tin. Because they always said if a mouse found your snap he'd start eating it, then piddle on it so you'd have to throw the rest away and he could have it later. When I first went down, we had tubs to take the coal out the pit. And everybody broke up for a fortnight's holiday then. They don't now at Daw Mill. We used to put a plank up and put some bread in a tub. The mice'd go up the plank, fall in the tub and couldn't get out. After the fortnight, the tub would be full of dead mice when we come back.'

Although the mice could be a nuisance, they were also a good sign, according to John Moffat. 'Mice are everywhere in pits. Mice will come out and sit by you while you eat your snap, especially after a pit shutdown. If there's no mice in a pit, then you get out. There's trouble coming.'

John worked at Baddesley and now works at Daw Mill, a very modern colliery. But even there, mice are to be found. And because there was a drift there – an inclined entrance – other creatures would venture in. 'There's a drift at Daw Mill, and we've had a squirrel and an owl down the drift. There'd be rats round the pit yard, but I never saw any underground.'

Bill Joyce told me of other creatures that featured at Coventry pit. 'We didn't have much trouble with mice, but the flies! Flies was the big thing down Keresley pit. We used to reckon that's where they all went in the winter. Them great big houseflies, with a big red nose. Plus there were thousands of crickets.

'We had an inspector used to come down. He lived up the village, in one of the special houses they built for managers and such. He came down one day, and we were having our snap. The flies used to swarm round. It was hot, red hot, about 90°. The sweat used to pour out of you. We only worked in shorts, socks and boots. It was electric lights at this time, and we used to take the headlamp off, and put it down. We used to get a shovel of dirt, loose dirt. We'd put a piece of bread, wet bread, on a piece of

Men using a shearer on the coalface at Coventry colliery. (National Archives)

119

paper, with all the lights shining on it. And within about five minutes that would be absolutely covered in flies. I'm not talking about tens, I'm talking about hundreds.

'This inspector happened to come down, and he says, "What's that?" I says, "Don't disturb it, it's the flies." He says, "You were at a meeting with me and the manager last week, and you were complaining about the filth and the flies, and here you are, you're feeding them! I'm not very pleased at all with this." I says, "Don't get worried." "Worried?" he said, "I'm devastated. I'm absolutely surprised at you, Bill Joyce." "Now," I said, "there's a reason. Show him, Horace." Up Horace gets, with a big shovelful of dust. I said to the inspector, "Now shine a light on that, and if one of those flies gets away, I'll give you five pounds." "And I'll take it!" he said. "Get the lights round here. I don't want to miss one."

'They all stood round with their lights shining on this bit of paper with flies all over it. Horace drops the dust on top, and I jumped on. "Bang!" I said, "How many's got out?" He was looking. He got his stick, poking in the dust. "Well, I wouldn't believe it," he said. And funnily enough, at the next management meeting we went to, he stood and announced what we'd done. "I was really surprised," he said. "I was annoyed with 'em, but it really worked." And I'm not kidding you if there wasn't two hundred flies there. Two hundred in one swipe.'

Ponies, mice, flies, crickets and the odd owl and squirrel. The miners were certainly not short of live companions down the pit.

Chapter 10

Lid Kids and Other Career Moves

One interesting aspect of my conversations with Warwickshire miners was hearing about the jobs they had done at various pits, and the story of their careers in the mining industry.

What on earth was a 'Lid Kid'? Peter Goodridge recalled, 'I was at Baddesley for about thirteen and a half years. When I first went down, at eighteen, I started off on supplies. We were unloading supplies on the left-hand rip on 21s, and the deputy, Harold Wood, came along with the under-manager. Mr Welford spotted me and he says to Harold, "I want this lad on the coalface."

'The next day, Harold says, "Come on, you're on the face, you're bar dragging." Well, that was keeping the coalface strippers supplied with their props and bars and lids and everything. The lids were the pads that went between the prop and the bar. They were called pads at most pits, but at Baddesley they were called lids. So my informal title was the Lid Kid. I was the Lid Kid for about twelve months.

'The best thing about this was that the men said to me, "Wait on the bridge on Friday." This bridge was over the reservoir. The men drew their pay and they had to go over the bridge. And it was the practice for the Lid Kid to get a tip, as long as he'd looked after the men properly and kept them well supplied. The going rate was two bob from each man. There were twenty-five strippers in each end, so I finished up with two pounds ten shillings. And the best of it was, there was one end on the day shift one week, the other end was day shift the next week, and on the third week both ends were on days. So that week, there were fifty strippers on the face. I'd have to rush around like something gone mad to do the job, to keep them supplied. So that week I was getting a fiver in tips, which was equal to my wages. That was the Lid Kid's job.'

Peter had an interesting, if chequered, career in the mining industry. He did his coalface training, and his 'moving-up' training. 'In a lot of pits it was called pan moving. What it was, it was moving the conveyor out after the strippers had finished and cleared a new track – moving the conveyor over into the new track. I did that for about ten years. Then I had quite a bad back injury caused by lifting a hydraulic prop. I must have lifted it awkwardly or lifted it too suddenly. Luckily, there was a deputy's course just starting at North Warwickshire College in Nuneaton, and I got permission to go onto it.

'So I did my deputy's course, and started as a shot-firer. I must have done some decent work because the course tutor, Frank Harrison, said, "Have you ever thought of carrying on studying?" I hadn't but I said that I'd be interested. There was a three-year mining engineering national day release course. So I did that and got my national certificate in mining engineering. This all happened while I was at Baddesley.

'Ted Hughes, the manager at Baddesley, he had me up in the office. And I thought, "Oh God, what have I done now?" because the overman used to take a delight in picking on me, and I suppose

I was a bit neurotic about it. He resented me having what he said was a day off a week. Anyway, Ted Hughes had me up the office, and he said, "I know you've been studying, getting qualifications, but you won't get on at this pit. I have spoken to my colleague at Daw Mill, Bill Chambers, and he's agreed to take you under his wing, if you want to go."

'So it had been arranged for me to go to Dexter. It was the Dexter end of Daw Mill. It was the same pit, but the men at the Dexter end still went up and down the Dexter shaft. I went there as a shot-firer at first, but I went to deputy straight away. I was shot firing for a couple of weeks in 7s west, which was the coalface at the Dexter end, but then a couple of weeks later, Les Forsythe, the 7s outbye deputy, got a job in the control room at Daw Mill. So that left his job vacant, and they gave it to me.

'I had eighteen months there as 7s outbye deputy. Also on the district was 40s developments. I had to look after them as well,

The headgear and winding house at Dexter colliery. (National Archives)

Dexter colliery: a miner checking the picks on the shearer drum of the trepanner. (National Archives)

and do the shot firing and everything. I was looking for promotion and Kingsbury colliery were advertising for an overman. Bill Chambers had asked me not to go. He said, "You stay here. This is a pit with a future." Which, of course, it was. Daw Mill is still producing coal and breaking all records. But I said, "No. I think I'd be better to start as an overman at another pit."

'I went to Kingsbury – this was in 1966 – and I was there three months. I didn't like the place. The men were all right, my overman colleagues were okay, but I didn't get on with the manager. One day he came round my district, found fault with everything and gave me such a roasting. So I went home that night and I said to Carol, "I've had enough." So I took my resignation in the next day, even though I hadn't got a job to go to. That was it, my career in the mining industry over.'

Peter took a job as a storesman at a nearby garage – Smiths Garage in Pinwall. When the Open University started in 1971, he enrolled and graduated in 1975. He taught part-time for twelve months at North Warwickshire College, teaching English and Commerce. The job then became full-time. Between 1975 and 1980, Peter did his Cert Ed, and an Open University honours degree. After a period as Director of Youth Training, he became head of Management Studies until he took early retirement in 1990 – a satisfying academic career, and all because he didn't get on with the manager at Kingsbury pit.

Bill Joyce's life in mining was more straightforward. When he came out of the army in 1948, he went down Coventry pit, intending to stay there for just eighteen months, and he retired after nearly forty years in the same pit. Bill recalled, 'In those days, you had to start from the bottom, and gradually do every job, working inbye until you got onto the coalface.

'Then you did two years on what they called 'getting' – learning the face work with an older chap. You had to learn all the dangers, the timbering, the packing, the way of strengthening girders. You'd go all through the jobs. When you'd done that, you'd be signed on as a contractor. Now a contractor wasn't like

Setting girders at Daw Mill colliery. (National Archives)

a miner is today. You were a special person in your own right, and you could be sent to any job. You worked in gangs, five or six to a coalface. But they could take you off that one, and put you on another one. In those days, it was all shovel and pick – hand work – there was no cutting as such. And you were only paid for what you did.'

Bill went on, 'Coventry was a different colliery because you had a 26-ft-thick coal seam. They used to work that as one seam, but there was so many killed that the government inspectors stopped it. Then they had teams of specialists looking at different ways of working it. They came up with an idea of working it in three tiers.

'So what they did, they worked it on what they called the return – the retreat method. They'd drive down for fourteen hundred yards – it was all downhill – and then work back, retreat. All your

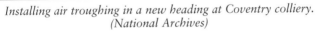

Installing air troughing in a new heading at Coventry colliery.
(National Archives)

Coventry colliery: winching the cradle up. (National Archives)

troubles were left behind you. You took eight foot. You went up for about fifty or sixty yards, and by that time the back, all above you, was dropping down. So then they went back and they drove up there, and took another six foot. And that advanced at the same speed as what the front one was going. The first one was called the Slate coal, the second one was the Rider, which rode on the back of the Slate. They done the same thing forty yards up, and they went for the last six foot, which was called the Two-Yard. They advanced up that way as three seams, until they got to the top.'

In the 1970s Bill damaged his back, and was out for seven or eight months. He saw a specialist who told him he hadn't got to go down the pit again. However, Bill met an old mate who told him about a man who had cured his back problem. 'He told me he'd been to a chap who was one of these bone-menders, as we called them. He told me that this bone-mender did all the professional wrestlers. I got the address off him and I went to Leicester to see him. And he put me right. He'd been a master butcher in his early life, so he knew all the bones of the animals. He worked on me for about twenty minutes. "Right," he says, "are you working?" I said, "I haven't worked for seven months, since I had the accident. I've had to come here on the bus – I couldn't drive." "Well, you can go back to work next week," he says. "Where do you work?" I says, "At the coalface." "Oh," he says, "well, in that case, have another two weeks off."

'I went back down the pit, working, for a good few years. I had a back support on, a steel corset. Then I came up on the bank because I'd smashed my thumb, smashed my arm, my shoulder, my head.

'So I come out and I seen my manager, and I told him. And he says, "Would you come on the bank, in charge, on the afternoon shift. There's a swivel chair. You'll be able to sit down, and your experience will get you through." Because I had taught a lot of people. On the bank, in that control room you were in charge. The management would go off at about five o'clock, and there was only you there until the night-shift under-manager come on. So he had to make me up to something, to give me that little bit of authority, so I was made an overman when I came on the bank.' Bill told me he'd been offered a post of overman while he was working underground but he'd turned it down. 'When they said I didn't get paid for weekends, I said, "If I'm working, I want to get paid for it."

'When I was on the bank, I once said, "I've had a change of position. I've got three hundred men under me. Once the management have gone home, I'm in charge, and the three hundred men under me are the afternoon shift once they've gone down!" If they were underground, they were all under me, weren't they?'

Bill is now retired and has found a wonderful hobby – painting in oils. I have seen his paintings, and one thing that struck me was the subject of his pictures. There were birds of prey, country scenes, cottages, woods: all in the countryside and all above

Some of the superb oil paintings by Coventry miner Bill Joyce.

ground. There wasn't a single picture of life underground. That he has left behind.

John Moffat started at Baddesley pit in 1970, and became a deputy there in 1986. Three years later he moved to Daw Mill again as a deputy, but in 1990 he was promoted to overman. He told me, 'I was an overman from the '90s until I took this job as full-time NACODS secretary. I had to be voted in, and the vote comes every two years. It's staggered so it's the branch secretary elected one year, and the branch president the other year. I'll have put up for re-election every two years.'

Good friends Malcolm Beck and Ev Emery were both in what was known as the power group, Malc being an electrician and Ev a fitter. Malc started at Newdigate in 1970 as an apprentice electrician and, having served his time, he went down the pit working in a heading with Ev. In 1982 both Malc and Ev finished at Newdigate and moved to Daw Mill. Malc told me, 'They called us the Boat People when we went to Daw Mill, like we were

Daw Mill: cages at the shaft top. (National Archives)

refugees sailing in from another country.' He worked there until April 2010 with just short of thirty years in mining. 'I ended up on the bloody face, the last ten years. I preferred the headings, because there's not so much pressure, but for whatever reason you end up on the face.

'And it's a culture change then, especially at Daw Mill because you were expected to do overtime every shift. It goes with the job. It's good money, don't get me wrong, but you're expected to stop there till the other shift come on. You do get used to it, eventually, but it's a bit of a bind. We were on three shifts: nights, afternoons and days, which is horrendous. I couldn't get on with nights. I didn't like days much. The best shift for me was the afternoon shift, the old man's shift as they used to call it. That's 12 till 7. It's a cracking shift, if you didn't have to stop overtime.

'I've been retired ever since, and I'm thoroughly enjoying it. And I love this shift pattern, the one I'm on at the minute! It's brilliant.'

Ev had come to Newdigate after working twelve years at Haunchwood and one at Arley. He told me, 'I was a fitter down the pit, doing shifts on headings at the end. Unfortunately, I lost the wife and I was left with two girls, 18 and 13. We had a decent engineer at the time, and he asked if he could do anything for me. Well, with two girls of that age, I wanted to go on days regular instead of shifts. So that's when I come onto the job I'm doing now, looking after all the lifting equipment. We assemble our own chains and look after the lifting equipment. I've done that job ever since, and I get pleasure out of it. So I still go to work. Because if I sat at home, I'd be sitting on my own, so I might as well go and sit at work with the lads, and have a cup of coffee and do a bit of work.'

Yes, Ev did say '... *the job I'm doing now*'! Now in his seventies, he began working down the pit in 1955, and is still working as a fitter at Daw Mill, which I think is incredible. He commented, 'It has a bit of purpose, because it keeps running my car. That's my fifth Jag outside. I always wanted a Jag. I've always worked – I can't remember the last time I was on the box, touch wood. I've been a regular worker. I worked overtime when I was

Daw Mill: arriving at the pit. (National Archives)

younger, with a family, but I just go five days now, just to keep the food on the table and keep active. You've got to keep active in your seventies.'

Malc told me, 'It was very cosmopolitan at Daw Mill. They even come in from Welbeck in Notts. But Daw Mill didn't have any men from Coventry. Daw Mill wouldn't have any from Coventry when they shut, because they were strong NUM. Daw Mill is a huge pit compared with what we were used to. Newdigate, Arley, they were little pits with little roadways, whereas at Daw Mill, the seam is four and five metres high. I mean, I couldn't believe it, the first time I went on the face at Daw Mill. I thought, "Oh my god, what's this?" I just could not believe it, compared with the struggles we had at Newdigate. But you think, "I can see why they shut these little jacky pits like Newdigate." We called them jacky pits – little pits. You can see why they shut pits like that when you've got this huge mass of coal that you can go for, and get it

This monument at the village of Piccadilly commemorates miners who worked at Kingsbury and Dexter collieries.

easily. Whereas in the jacky pits, you were shovelling on your hands and knees – it's just not on really.'

Howard Baker began in 1950, and did three years at Kingsbury colliery, but all the while studying mining engineering for one day a week. Howard explained, 'From then, I went on a sandwich course – six months on and six months off. That's six months at Cannock Tech and six months at the pit, getting your practical. All the people from the West Midlands – North Staffs, South Staffs and Warwickshire – went to Cannock. I did that for two years, and the final year was a nine-month course at Stoke-on-Trent. At the end of that you took your first class Certificate of Competency – that's a manager's qualification – and you took your exam to get into the Institute of Mining Engineers.

'Next I did two years on a scheme which introduced you to area office, financial department, purchasing and stores, things like that. And then it was a matter of making sure you'd got all your experience on a coalface. I went back to Kingsbury for all that. As

---

Many of the bricks on the wall of the monument carry the names of miners.

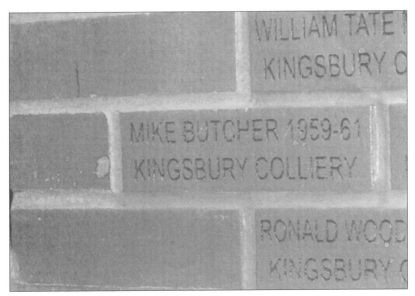

soon as I'd got sufficient experience in for coalface work, I could take the shot-firer's and deputy's papers. Then you moved from the NUM – the National Union of Miners – into NACODS – the National Association of Colliery Overmen, Deputies and Shotfirers.

'I went for a very short time to Birch Coppice as a shot-firer. I didn't work there many months, before I went to Binley colliery, the other side of Coventry. I went there as a supplies overman. I didn't actually ever work as a deputy – I went from being a shot-firer straight to being a supplies overman. I hadn't been there too long before I moved off that onto the production side. I went to Binley in about 1957, and then I went to Newdigate. I went there as an assistant to the manager – that was a new post primarily for people like me who were working their way up. I did two years at Newdigate, and then I went to Daw Mill in 1964 as under-manager. I was at Daw Mill from 1964–71, and then another

Birch Coppice colliery, December 1973. (National Archives)

Electric driller at work at Birch Coppice. The drill was known as a 'bull's head'. (National Archives)

short spell as the deputy manager at Newdigate, and then I went to Keresley. I was at Keresley for a few years as deputy manager. A deputy manager is higher than an under-manager but junior to the manager.' Howard finished his career by leaving Warwickshire and going to a Leicestershire colliery as a deputy manager for the rest of his time.

Bill Joyce and Ken Lewis – known as Boyo – worked together at Coventry colliery. Bill is now a talented painter, and Ken is a fine poet. As ever, Ken summed up his thoughts in a wonderful poem that he calls *Retirement 85*:

> *At last I've finished at the pit*
> *How time is passing by*
> *Old memories flood back to me*
> *A tear comes to my eye.*
>
> *To think of all those bygone years*
> *Some of pleasure, some of pain*
> *Riding up and down the shaft*
> *Never to ride again.*
>
> *I started forty years ago*
> *It seems like yesterday*
> *The work was ten times harder then*
> *With not a lot of pay.*
>
> *To put on a helmet and nailly boots*
> *Was a big thing for most of the lads*
> *To dress like your dad would make you feel great*
> *To walk up to the pit in knee pads.*
>
> *We grew up the hard way, with shovel in hand,*
> *Working through hardship and pains*
> *It's nice to sit back now and think of those times*
> *In the short space of life that remains.*

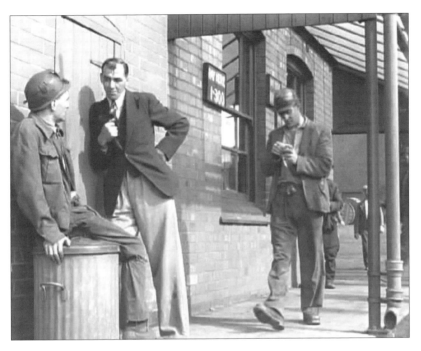

A miner counting his wages at Haunchwood colliery.

To get out of bed at six o'clock
And fill up your snap tin and flask
You would try to defy the ache in your back
As you strode up the hill to your task.

Then at the pit shaft, you queue to go down
Down in the earth far below
A feeling of comradeship hard to describe
Would fill your insides with a glow.

You glance at the big stones that hang overhead
The chance is, they're not going to fall
Some chances that you've got to take through your life
Makes you think, Was it worth it at all?

A group of miners at Haunchwood. (National Archives)

Sometimes you cough and retch in the night
Your lungs would feel full up with dust
But when the alarm clock rings clearly out
You don't want to get up, but you must.

Now all those memories are left far behind
All of them good times and bad
Memories that linger when you were eighteen
To be part of those times makes me sad.

Well now, I've finished, my task it is done
I have tried to put memories to rhyme
Goodbye to the coal dust, goodbye to the pit
My tools on the ratch for all time.

Glossary

Afterdamp: a deadly mixture which could occur after an explosion.

Baiting or Dinting: digging up the floor of a roadway.

Bank: the surface area of a colliery. I did once meet a miner who was in charge of the surface area, who insisted on writing 'bank manager' after his signature!

Black Damp: carbon dioxide

Chocks: wooden blocks of wood, roughly used to support the roof of the coalface.

Downcast shaft: for men and materials and fresh air.

Dowty: a hand-operated hydraulic prop.

Drift: a sloping roadway used to access lower or higher areas. A drift mine was a pit where there was no shaft, and miners would walk down into the mine.

Firedamp: a mixture of methane gas and air. The most dangerous mixture is when the proportion of methane is between 5% and 15%, and so an explosion is possible.

Gates: roadways leading to and from a face.

Gob: waste. Also the area behind the face chocks where the coal had been removed, and waste was stored.

Hardstop: plaster used to form a sealant.

Headings: roadways which are being developed, moving forward to open up new faces.

Inbye: travelling underground from the pit bottom to the face.

Jacky pit: a very small pit.

Keps: steel blocks which were moved into a shaft under the cage bottom, for the cage to rest on.

Main Gate: the intake airway which was the conveyor belt road down which the coal travelled.

Onsetter: the man in charge in the pit bottom, seeing to the loading and unloading of coal and men.

Ostler: the man in charge of the pit ponies.

Outbye: travelling from the coalface back to the pit bottom.

Pit Bottom: the area of the pit at the bottom of the shaft, and therefore the first area reached by a visitor.

Props/Trees: wooden supports holding up the roof. In Warwickshire pits, props were often called trees.

Return Airway: a roadway along which air returns from the working face.

Ring: an arched girder which supported the roof. A ring consisted of two legs and a crown.

Self Rescuer: a stainless steel canister, about the size of a small tea caddy, carried by the miner at all times. It contained a small respirator with a mouthpiece, nose clip and webbing straps to hold it in place. Also an air cooler, smoke and dust filters, and a substance called hopcalite, which converts carbon monoxide into carbon dioxide. They're supposed to last for an hour.

Shearer: machine used to cut coal on a longwall face.

Shift: the part of any day worked, i.e. days, afternoons or nights.

Shotfirer: person in charge of explosives.

Snap: sandwiches, etc, taken down the pit for eating during a break.

Sump: the bottom of a shaft, or any other place in a mine, that is used as a collecting point for drainage water.

Tail Gate: the majority of the face supplies are transported via this roadway. Also known as the return or supply gate.

Trambulance: a stretcher on wheels.

Unions: The main union for mineworkers was the NUM (National Union of Miners). Electricians and fitters had their own section – the Power Group – within the NUM. Clerical workers at the pit were members of COSA, which was affiliated to the NUM. The UDM (Union of Democratic Miners) was formed after the 1984/5 strike by those miners who had not supported the strike. Originally the UDM was based in Nottinghamshire, but when the pits were privatised in 1994, the new owners insisted that their men should join the UDM, as they believed that the UDM would be less militant. (The UDM is described by NUM loyalists as 'the scab union' or 'the bosses' union'.) NACODS is the union of colliery overmen, deputies and shotfirers. BACM (British Association of Colliery Management) was the union for colliery managers and undermanagers.

Upcast Shaft: shaft through which air returns to the surface after ventilating the mine workings, for coal winding and returned air.

Water Rats: old name for men who worked on pumps to keep the pits free of flooding.

Index